Writing for Science Students

Palgrave Study Skills

Business Degree Success
Career Skills
Cite Them Right (10th edn)
Critical Thinking Skills (3rd edn)
Dissertations and Project Reports
e-Learning Skills (2nd edn)
The Exam Skills Handbook (2nd edn)
Get Sorted
The Graduate Career Guidebook
Great Ways to Learn Anatomy and Physiology
  (2nd edn)
How to Begin Studying English Literature (4th edn)
How to Study Foreign Languages
How to Study Linguistics (2nd edn)
How to Use Your Reading in Your Essays (2nd edn)
How to Write Better Essays (3rd edn)
How to Write Your Undergraduate Dissertation
  (2nd edn)
Improve Your Grammar (2nd edn)
Information Skills
The International Student Handbook
The Mature Student's Guide to Writing (3rd edn)
The Mature Student's Handbook
The Palgrave Student Planner
The Personal Tutor's Handbook
Practical Criticism
Presentation Skills for Students (3rd edn)
The Principles of Writing in Psychology
Professional Writing (3rd edn)
Researching Online
Skills for Success (3rd edn)
Smart Thinking
The Student's Guide to Writing (3rd edn)
The Student Phrase Book
Study Skills Connected
Study Skills for International Postgraduates
Study Skills for Speakers of English as a Second
  Language
The Study Skills Handbook (4th edn)
Studying History (3rd edn)

Studying Law (4th edn)
Studying Modern Drama (2nd edn)
Studying Psychology (2nd edn)
Success in Academic Writing
Teaching Study Skills and Supporting Learning
The Undergraduate Research Handbook
The Work-Based Learning Student Handbook
  (2nd edn)
Work Placements – A Survival Guide for Students
Write it Right (2nd edn)
Writing for Engineers (3rd edn)
Writing for Law
Writing for Nursing and Midwifery Students
  (2nd edn)
Writing History Essays (2nd edn)
You2Uni: Decide. Prepare. Apply

Pocket Study Skills

14 Days to Exam Success
Analyzing a Case Study
Brilliant Writing Tips for Students
Completing Your PhD
Doing Research
Getting Critical (2nd edn)
Planning Your Dissertation
Planning Your Essay (2nd edn)
Planning Your PhD
Posters and Presentations
Reading and Making Notes (2nd edn)
Referencing and Understanding Plagiarism
Reflective Writing
Report Writing
Science Study Skills
Studying with Dyslexia
Success in Groupwork
Time Management
Where's Your Argument?
Writing for University (2nd edn)

Palgrave Career Skills

Excel at Graduate Interviews

Writing for Science Students

Jennifer Boyle and Scott Ramsay

 macmillan education palgrave

First published 2017 by
PALGRAVE

Palgrave in the UK is an imprint of Macmillan Publishers Limited, registered in England, company number 785998, of 4 Crinan Street, London, N1 9XW.

Palgrave® and Macmillan® are registered trademarks in the United States, the United Kingdom, Europe and other countries.

ISBN 978–1–137–57151–9 paperback

This book is printed on paper suitable for recycling and made from fully managed and sustained forest sources. Logging, pulping and manufacturing processes are expected to conform to the environmental regulations of the country of origin.

A catalogue record for this book is available from the British Library.

A catalog record for this book is available from the Library of Congress.

Printed in China

Table of Contents

List of Figures

List of Tables

List of Boxes

Acknowledgments

In writing this book, we consulted with many colleagues, both at the University of Glasgow and beyond. In particular, we would like to thank Dr Chris Finlay and Dr Mary McVey from the School of Life Sciences, and Dr Eric Yao from the School of Physics and Astronomy. The experiences they shared of grading and giving feedback to large first-year classes were instrumental in shaping the sections of the book that orient readers with the expectations of a marker. Additionally, their feedback on our critical analysis chapter was indispensable.

We would also like to thank Dr Amanda Sykes and, from Edinburgh Napier University, Dr Anne Tierney, prior collaborations with whom formed the basis for our advice on how to incorporate other people's work.

Another long-time classroom collaborator, Heather Worlledge-Andrew, helped to inform the chapters on finding materials. As a former Subject Librarian for the College of Medical, Veterinary and Life Sciences at the University of Glasgow, the experience she has shared over the years in the intricacies of how to sensibly find and access journal articles was invaluable.

Finally, we would like to thank our PhD supervisors, Dr Peter Dominy and Dr Marilyn Dunn, who played such a large part in helping us to shape our own writing styles during the course of writing our PhD dissertations.

Introduction

Top 3 staff comments on scientific writing:

► We offer guidance on writing in class, but until students actually have a go at it themselves, it still seems natural that they will panic.
► Overall quality of written work is often poor, which is frustrating when we can see that the students have the necessary scientific knowledge. We can't give full marks.
► Lab reports are the classic example of what 'scientific writing' means, but they make up only a very small part of a successful scientist's written output.

Top 3 student comments on scientific writing:

► I didn't really enjoy English at school, so I'm not looking forward to having to write.
► The structure and format confuses me – what information should go where?
► It's hard to express complicated things clearly without just quoting from someone else.

Pick up this book if you want something designed to meet the specific needs of science students. There are plenty of writing guides for the university audience, but most of them cater to students who spend their whole lives writing essays: students in the arts and the humanities. Scientific degrees don't work that way, and scientific writing doesn't look the same as theirs.

This book actively works to give you an understanding of scientific writing from start to finish, and an understanding of what your markers want. It's divided into three sections: Understanding Scientific Writing, Preparing to Write, and Getting Down to Writing. The sections are designed to take you through every stage of the writing process, from understanding the assignment you've been set, to researching and planning, right through to drafting and editing.

Where relevant, we've incorporated example scientific sentences and paragraphs to help illustrate our points and solidify your understanding.

Our approach puts you in charge of your writing by explaining why we write in a certain way in the sciences, instead of issuing rules and demands which might seem arbitrary and confusing. A grasp of clear, concise writing is just as relevant and achievable for science students as those in any other discipline. Your preference for scientific simplicity and rigour is what makes you an ideal scientific writer, and we'll show you how to capitalise on that.

As your degree goes on, you'll spend more and more time reading scientific journal articles to widen your knowledge. We'll show you how to put in place strategies and systems at the research stage to make your eventual writing much easier. You'll also be doing your own research in labs, so we'll give you pointers on how to choose the best of your practical work to put into your write-ups and dissertations. And when you're incorporating other people's work, whether it's lecture material, information from textbooks or scientific articles, or your own conclusions, we'll show you how to properly cite and reference all these different sources in the same way that professional scientists do.

We both work every day with students, from first-year to PhD level. Often, those students come to see us when they want to improve their work, or have problems they need to iron out. As such, we're familiar with the type of questions you're likely to ask. We also work every day with staff who want to think about the best way to set assignments for their students, or deliver effective feedback. This means we have a good idea of where miscommunications can occur, and how to help you better understand what your tutors want to see you demonstrate in your written work. We'll open each chapter with a list of top three issues from students and staff to give you an idea of what to expect and put your own questions in context. Everything we've written hangs around our collective experience of teaching students about writing at degree level in the British university system.

While it is true that science students often feel anxious about their writing, we can honestly tell you that they are also among the best writers we work with. We hope that this book will give you the knowledge you need to feel confident about your skills as a writer, and about your ability to express your knowledge and understanding through your reports, essays, and dissertations.

Why you'll enjoy scientific writing

If you're anything like most students we see, you gravitated towards the sciences in high school because you appreciated the predictability, the rules, and the emphasis on doing something practical. You might have been interested in discovering something that no-one has ever known before. You might just enjoy doing experiments to see what happens. I doubt that many, if any, of you chose your science subject because you wanted to write about it. Writing seemed like a necessary evil, and something that was only important in the arts subjects.

English literature was the class for analysing texts and writing essays in response. It was the subject where *what* you said and *how* you said it were equally important. Discursive writing, critical evaluations, close readings, creative writing – these are all things you probably would have *had* to do, and which you probably thought had little relevance to the way we do science.

That perception is largely correct, but you do need to spend a little time becoming good at the other kinds of writing we do have to do in science. The good news is that scientific writing is easier than its artistic equivalent.

The reasons that you were attracted to science are the same reasons you'll find the writing quite simple to do. Do you enjoy logic? The way your academic writing should be laid out follows a systematic pattern – introduction, methodology, what you find, and then what this means. To deviate from that order would be to break the chain of logical causality (that is, putting things in an order where what comes next can be explained by what went before). Do you appreciate simplicity? The style of sentences favoured in most sections of university-level report writing is that of short, direct presentation of facts and interpretations. Do you appreciate objectivity? The sections of your writing where you present facts and the sections where you discuss your interpretation of them are kept separate, meaning it is easy for your reader to first make up their own mind based on the results, and then check this against your conclusion.

In short, you don't need to learn any new creative skill to become an excellent scientific writer. We're here to help you refine the inclinations and preferences you already have so that you can make sure your writing is as clear and well-grounded as possible.

What makes it different

Let's expand a bit more on the difference between high school English literature essays and university-level science writing. We'll put lab reports aside for the moment, as that kind of writing doesn't happen in English literature and so it'll be easier to compare essays with essays.

The challenge for a student writing an essay in English literature is to engage with the source text and think in the abstract. That means the subject matter is not tangible, not physical. While the sciences are primarily observational, the arts are based on interpretation. For example, a novelist might use weather as a metaphor to reflect the emotional development of their characters, and in a discursive essay about the different ways they do this, the outcome being analysed (the depiction of the characters' emotions) has a large element of subjectivity. Rain might be interpreted by one student as a symbol of depression, while another might see it as a symbol of cleansing and renewal. As long as either position was argued convincingly, fully, with examples from the text, each essay could potentially score high marks.

Without asking the novelist, we can never know for sure. Even after asking them, there would be those who would still argue their own interpretation. 'If someone tells you what a story is about, they are probably right. If they tell you that that is *all* the story is about, they are very definitely wrong' (Gaiman, 2013). But getting to 'the truth' isn't really the point of English literature essays, and that's why they can be difficult to create.

Scientific essays, on the other hand, should always be based on objective observations and conclusions. You can begin simply as a reporter of what you observe, combine pieces of knowledge in response to a question, and build from there. Since your essays won't be based on your own scientific work, the term 'objective observations' in this instance means the observations you hear about from textbooks, lectures, and from reading scientific journal articles.

Let's take an example of a typical essay task in sciences.

If you're asked in an essay question to compare and contrast two things, the most logical way would be to properly explain thing A, then properly explain thing B, then move on to a comparison between what you've just laid out. This is simple and straightforward, albeit a little basic.

You could probably improve on such a structure by breaking down the pros and cons of thing A and thing B into categories, which you can then deal with in their own paragraphs. You may open your essay with an introduction telling the reader what topics they can expect to read about, then give a very brief introduction to A and B, before moving on to spend most of the essay comparing A and B on the basis of these categories you just identified.

For example, if you were comparing lab techniques, you might open with a brief explanation of what each technique is for and its key features, then move into the main body of your essay where the comparison happens. The first paragraph of the main body might be about the relative speeds of each technique; speed is therefore your first category. Next might be a paragraph about another category – cost. A third paragraph might deal with the availability of the raw materials needed for each technique. Each of these three categories deserves at least its own separate paragraph, or perhaps more, depending on the word count of your assignment and thus how much detail you can go into. You may then choose to conclude by making a recommendation based on all the factors you've discussed. This would demonstrate an awareness of why this was an interesting comparison to make in the first place, and show that you've thought deeply about it.

The important point we're making here is that you don't need to do anything particularly complex in order to pull off a highly scoring essay in science. You just need to be clear, to have a structure which is easy for your reader to make sense of, and to use evidence from your further reading, where appropriate. (You can read more about these last two points in Chapter 11 – Producing a Draft and Building Your Argument, and Chapter 8 – Incorporating and Referencing Other People's Work.)

When you reach the later stages of your degree, it will be increasingly important that you show your reader/marker that you are capable of interpretation, as well as just repeating what you know. This skill is commonly called 'critical analysis'. Others call it 'demonstrating original thought'. Some will refer to it as 'evaluation and synthesis' – evaluation of the facts you've presented and synthesis of your own thoughts about them. It's important to draw another distinction here between what those terms mean in science as compared with your high school English literature classes.

'Original thought' to the people marking your work *does not* mean ideas that no-one on the planet has ever had before. If you're writing about objectively true facts, discovered by other people at some point in the past, and if those findings are available in a journal for all to see, then it's unavoidable that many people will already have seen them and come to the same interpretations as you. That doesn't matter at all. In this context, 'original' does not mean the same as 'unique'. Instead, it means that your interpretations should have occurred to you on your own, without anyone passing them on to you. (In fact, if science were perfectly objective and reproducible, then everyone should be able to look at any scientific body of evidence and have *exactly the same* original interpretation.)

Lab reports don't have a direct comparison in English classes, but the principles we've mentioned here still hold true: you need to be logical with the sequence in which you describe your methods; you need to report your findings fully before you can begin to walk your reader through an interpretation of them (thus your results section should be separate from, and prior to, your conclusions section); and you need to show evidence of your own thinking at the end. This is often overlooked by students: you must make an effort to relate your findings back to the theory and the existing knowledge base you mentioned in your introduction if you want to achieve a high mark. None of this requires unique, never-thought-of-before analysis, and none of it depends upon a command of pretentious language.

Scientific writing may not be immediately easy to master, but it is undeniably simple to learn.

Rules, conventions, and why we have them

The rules and standard conventions of scientific writing echo the principles that underpin the scientific method itself. At their heart is the notion that every question is answerable, and that the answers to those questions are independent of the person who asks. By 'asking questions', we mean carrying out an investigation, experiment, or measurement. As we discover those answers, we add them to our collective understanding of how the world works, and we are generally happy to refer to these pieces of knowledge as facts.

A characteristic of a fact is that it should be the same to all observers, regardless of who they are. Different ways, or techniques, of answering a scientific question may of course lead to unexpectedly different answers. Two different labs who grow bacteria on Petri dishes with different manufacturers' nutrient mixtures could record different growth rates, for example, and this would make a crucial difference if you were investigating the life cycle of a new strain of an infectious agent. That's why we place so much importance on documenting the materials and the methods used in each experiment: if two people carry out the same experiment using the same method, they should truly arrive at the same result. The facts are the facts, the truth is the truth, and this is the case regardless of who the experimenters are.

This is the logical reasoning behind what we know today as scientific writing style, but the style itself didn't simply arise as a spontaneous trend in the scientific literature. It was created by the Royal Society, a body of scientists who first assembled in 1660 in London (and it's still around today, and you may recognise members of it among the lecturing staff at your university by the initials 'FRS' – Fellow of the Royal Society – after their name). One of the founding members, Thomas Sprat, made the case for avoiding the use of metaphors or impressive turns of phrase. His book serves as a guide for how new Royal Society members should conduct themselves, and in it he was quick to talk about the good work the Society had already done on formalising a system for clear scientific communication:

> It will suffice my present purpose, to point out, what has been done by the Royal Society [...] to reject all the amplifications, digressions, and swellings of style [...] They [the Royal Society] have exacted from all their members, a close, naked, natural way of speaking; positive expressions; clear senses. (Sprat, 1667, pp.113)

The principles envisaged by Sprat have been developed and refined over 450 years into the style of scientific writing we use today, giving us conventions such as using the past tense to describe experiments, and writing in the passive voice. These will be covered in more detail in Chapter 12 – Sounding Like a Scientist.

How these skills will help your future career

Scientific writing is a context-dependent language. We use it in academic settings – when writing lab reports, journal articles, and dissertations – in order to communicate with our peers. The ability to understand and use this style of writing is crucial in order to be successful in your studies.

The underlying principles of clarity and concision are useful beyond your time at university, no matter what career you decide to pursue. In non-science careers, as well as science careers, the ability to communicate clearly with an audience is vital and prized.

The ability to understand and reflect on writing itself as a means of communicating ideas will also enable you to adapt to different styles. For example, using a passive construction is standard in scientific writing because the passive emphasises the process over the person performing the process (this will be discussed in detail in Chapter 12). For example, 'The project was successfully managed.' However, this is totally unsuitable for CVs and job applications, where you need to draw attention to yourself, and use the active construction, 'I successfully managed the project.' Understanding how these styles differ will help you recognise when to use them, and how to use them effectively.

Conclusion

Having read this chapter, we hope that you will:

- have an understanding of how scientific writing is based around certain conventions and expectations;
- see writing positively as part of your skill set as a scientist;
- feel confident in your ability to *identify* high-quality scientific writing;
- feel optimistic that you can learn how to *produce* high-quality scientific writing.

Understanding Different Types of Scientific Writing

In the next chapters, we will look at five types, or genres, of scientific writing: lab reports, essays, dissertations, posters, and abstracts. This final type never exists on its own – abstracts are always a prelude to a much longer piece of writing – but no matter which genre of scientific writing they accompany, abstracts are broadly similar in whichever context they are used. For this reason, we've decided to give abstracts their own section.

If you have any questions about how university-level versions of these genres might differ from what you've had to produce before in high school or college, this chapter will help you figure out what to keep doing and what you need to build on. We know you'll be anxious to learn whether a school or college essay looks like a university essay, or whether your lab reports need to follow a different standard format. We'll show you here what your markers will expect yours to contain.

Universities are international places, so we recognise that many readers of this book will have come from different educational systems. If this describes you, then this chapter should also help you determine whether you need to redefine what you know as an 'essay' so that you can get your best possible grades from your markers here in the UK.

By the end of this part, we hope that you will:

- have an understanding of the purposes underlying each of these types of assignment: lab reports, essays, dissertations, posters, and abstracts;
- feel more confident in your ability to plan your own structure;
- be able to distinguish between a situation where it's important to relay procedural information (e.g. focus on experimental methods) and one where it's more important to discuss findings and implications;

- understand the difference between including information to demonstrate the breadth of research and being selective with the information so as to keep a coherent focus;
- think of formal structures, sections, and so on, as a guide to reader comprehension rather than a set of technical rules.

The Lab Report

Top 3 staff comments on lab reports:

▶ The methods haven't been fully explained / have been explained in far too much detail.
▶ The reason for doing this experiment isn't made clear, either in the introduction or the discussion.
▶ Good description of what was in the lab manual, but lacking in the discussion of the results.

Top 3 student comments on lab reports:

▶ Different markers tell me to focus on different sections for different reports, and I don't know which of them is right.
▶ I don't know if I should write in the past tense or the present, and in the active voice or the passive.
▶ Do I need references in a lab report?

Before we get into the details of what a lab report should or should not contain, we want to impress upon you the importance of understanding what your audience is looking for. You will likely have a series of labs over the duration of any given module. As such, your marker will have designed each lab for one or two main purposes, giving special thought to how these will benefit you. If you can identify the reasons for doing each lab, you might be able to improve your report by focusing your time and energy on demonstrating how you've developed in those most relevant aspects. This chapter will help you identify what those purposes might be, and will show you what information should (and should not) go into each section of a lab report.

Audience, purpose, and the standard lab report format

Sometimes the marker will have put a lab exercise into the curriculum so you can gain some knowledge about your subject. This might be done by way of a standard lab procedure designed to measure or create something entirely predictable, where only human or equipment error could lead you to a negative result. Sometimes they will have put them into the curriculum so you can get practice at a particular technique. Molecular biologists need to know how to pipette; animal and human biologists need to see how a skeleton articulates; physicists need to know how to operate standard detection equipment; chemists need to be confident with the operation of burettes and fine balances. Sometimes a lab will be on the curriculum because the experiments will be rich in data for you to record. Perhaps you'll end up measuring many different features of many individual samples, leading to a large and varied results section with lots of data types for you to manipulate. Sometimes labs will have been designed to challenge your ability to follow the scientific method. For example, labs in later years of degrees often begin with open questions, and you then have a chance to design and refine your own procedures (or 'protocols') based on the questions you alone are responsible for thinking up.

This isn't an exhaustive list of reasons that staff might put labs into your course, but in each of these different scenarios, the type of report you write may be quite different in substance and in the relative sizes of each section. Ask yourself if you can identify what seems to be most valuable to your marker, and consider whether to place more emphasis on this part of your report.

Your lab staff will also be able to give you a guide on this. They'll also be wary of giving you an unfair advantage, or of letting you coast. If you want to ask them for guidance, it's always a good idea to present your question as the result of some sensible thinking so as to avoid making yourself simply look like a needy student asking for more help than the rest of the class was given. This means you could say something considered and reflective, such as:

> I realise we've used a lot of new techniques in this lab and I'm wondering how that might feed into my report. Is that range one of the main things you want us to learn, and does that mean you're looking for us to write a really detailed explanation of each technique in the report? Or would you prefer us to say 'experiments were carried out according to the protocol in the lab manual' and dedicate more of our word count to writing about the results?

The most commonly used format for lab reports is the IMRaD report. **I**ntroduction, **M**aterials (and/or Methods), **R**esults, and **D**iscussion. Variations on this theme may feature on your course, perhaps with 'Discussion' either swapped or supplemented with a 'Conclusion' section, but it is unusual to see a report deviate widely from this outline. The format has been in use since around 1940 (at least in biomedical journals) when it took over from very descriptive types of articles (Sollaci and Pereira, 2004). It gradually increased in popularity until the 1970s, when it started to become formally recommended in journal guidelines as the style of preference, and it has stood the test of time over those last 45 years so that it is still with us today as the style of most scientists. This is testament to the way its clarity, its logical structure, and its separation of one type of information from the others has served the purposes of scientists: to allow readers to receive information and interpret it as objectively as possible.

Before we move into the finer details of how to actually build a report, we'll share with you the results of a study carried out by one of the authors of this book (Dr Scott Ramsay) along with a colleague, Dr Michael McEwan, also from the University of Glasgow's Learning & Teaching Centre. We surveyed staff who teach first-year students in chemistry, physics, and biology. We asked them to rate how well their students performed at various different aspects of writing lab reports, and what they perceived to be important. The main, overarching question in the survey was: 'What is the purpose of a lab report?', to which the respondents could select a maximum of three answers from the following options:

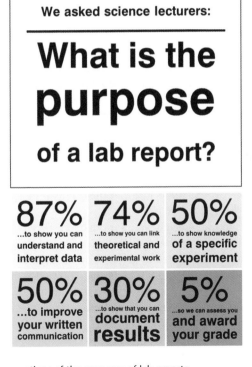

Figure 2.1   Staff perceptions of the purposes of lab reports

The most common answer – that 87% of staff are interested in your ability to interpret data – is probably not a surprise, but when 74% of lecturers say they're looking for evidence of a link between theory and experimental work, that's perhaps a bit less obvious. Yes, it seems like a reasonable thing to say, but how do you actually *do* that with your writing? Only 50% of staff said that you should learn about a specific experiment, so if you're ever confused and frustrated about why you've been told to carry one out when it seems like you'll never need to know how to do it again, rest assured that there are probably deeper skills connected to that lab that *are* important. Again, 50% said reports were there to improve your general communication skills. Only 5% of lecturers said the allocation of marks was a primary reason to give you this type of assignment, so don't just think of lab reports simply as a test.

In other results, the majority of staff said they didn't think first-year students were very confident about what was required of them, but they also said that lab reports were valuable for helping their students grasp the course material. With that in mind, let's look at what should (and shouldn't!) be in the different sections.

Introductions

Your introduction should justify your experiments to your reader. Why did you bother to do this work? What previous work was it based on? Was there a gap in our existing knowledge beforehand? Would answering an experimental question leave us better off somehow than we were before? Common justifications for experiments include economics, speed, efficiency, health, and, occasionally, pure scientific advancement. If you can say that the outcome of an experiment will allow us to do something more quickly, or more cost-effectively, or in a way that saves people's lives, your reader will buy into what you're saying and they'll be more motivated to read the rest of the report. How could they not, when you've just told them how important the knowledge will be?

As well as justifying the research, your introduction should clearly explain its theoretical underpinning. If you're investigating how food intake and exercise levels over the course of a week relate to the body weight and the fitness of your subjects, you will probably want to talk about our knowledge of the dietary and activity factors that influence whether someone remains healthy. It would strengthen your introduction to cite some literature (books, lecture slides, or published articles) that supports what you claim. Think carefully about the theory you include here because, as you've seen, markers will want to see you connect your eventual findings back to this in your conclusion section.

After setting out this background, your introduction should end with a statement of your aims. Try to avoid using clichéd phrases such as '*In this experiment*, X and Y will be measured and compared in order to determine Z'. Instead, go for a direct, concise statement about what will be done: 'In order to determine Z, X and Y will be measured and compared'. If you find yourself in a situation where you absolutely must mention the experiment itself, try to find a more sophisticated name for it. 'In this *investigation*', or 'For the purposes of this *study*' are more professional-sounding alternatives.

The most common question we are asked about the introduction is 'How many words should it take up?' This is a very difficult question to answer. Every discipline will have its own conventions, and some topics will demand a longer justification at the start than others. As a rule of thumb, though, aim to spend 10% of your word count on setting up the experiments for your reader. If you have a good reason to change this afterwards, do so.

Materials and methods

High school pupils are told that this section should allow your reader to repeat your experiments, should they ever need to. This is true, but in reality the materials and methods section is probably far more commonly used by a reader to check whether an experiment was done sensibly. It helps satisfy them that your attention to detail was adequate, that your processes were properly controlled so as to avoid errors, and that your methods were appropriate for any type of statistical interpretations you might have carried out. For example, you can use your methods section to detail your sample size and explain whether any decisions were made in advance about whether, and how, to identify vastly unusual data points in the course of your experiments and discard them from your analysis.

You should write your methods for the educated reader. They don't usually need to know whether you used a glass rod or a plastic one to stir your solution, or how your pH meter was calibrated before you used it. They *do* need to know that you stirred the solution, however, so they can be satisfied that the reactants were dispersed equally throughout the reaction vessel, and they *do* need to know if you measured the pH of your solution precisely with a properly calibrated electronic meter, rather than judging by eye with a rough measure like a litmus paper.

Sometimes, in the course of a lab practical, you will use the same basic method in every experiment, but you may tweak that method in order to generate every individual finding you describe in the results section later.

For example, you may take some plants and grow them all on the same type of soil, for the same length of time, under the same environmental conditions. You might then subject them to a high temperature to see how many of them survive. The basic method would be the same in each case, but you might heat some to 35°C, some to 40°C, and some to 45°C. If so, try to be concise about the standard elements of the procedure. You don't need a full history of the three different groups of plants. For example, it would be excessive to say:

> For experiment A, plants were grown at the standard growth temperature of 22°C for three weeks until mature, heated at 35°C for three hours, then returned to 22°C to recover. For experiment B, plants were also grown at the standard growth temperature of 22°C for three weeks until mature, then stressed at 40°C for three hours, then returned to 22°C to recover. For experiment C, plants were grown at a standard 22°C for three weeks until mature, then stressed at 45°C, then returned to 22°C to recover …

Instead, it's more concise to say:

> Plants were exposed to various heat stress regimes by first incubating in a temperature-controlled cabinet at 22°C for three weeks until maturity, then heating to one of a variety of stress temperatures for three hours, then recovering at 22°C again.

You can then explain all of the precise differences in temperature regimes in your results section later, as part of the paragraphs where you present each of the findings one-by-one. If there were many temperatures used, it may even be enough to mention these only in the axes, legends, and captions of whatever graphs you create from the dataset. The text of your results section should describe the data in a way that draws the reader's attention to the key findings. This means the results from the intermediate stress temperature may not be mentioned in the main text at all, if they would detract from your ability to communicate concisely.

Results

This is where you present your findings, bearing in mind the fundamental principle of objectivity. Your findings should consist of data completely separated from its interpretation. This is tricky at first, as it's common to be taught the standard mantra that 'each figure should be explained in the text'. This is true, but there's a subtle difference between explaining what a graphs *shows*, and saying what you think it *means*.

In an investigation into whether a structure would support a load of 1200 kg, it would be appropriate to plot a graph and then say something like 'This shows that the maximum safe loading weight for this platform is 975 kg', but it would *not* be appropriate to say 'This shows that the maximum safe loading weight for this platform is 975 kg, *and therefore a more robust platform would be required in order to withstand heavy use*'. This last piece of information is interpreting the data and relating it to a real-world scenario. That is the purpose of your discussion section, not your results. The only real exception to this would be if you discovered something so unusual that you had to re-evaluate the rationale or plan set out in your aims, and were forced to alter your next steps. If you think your reader would be unable to comprehend the next experiment without understanding the implications of the one before it, a brief justification lasting a sentence or two may be helpful between your presentation of the two results.

Chronology and flow

Your results should usually be presented in chronological order so that the reader can follow the process of everything you did from start to finish. Your marker is going to be educated to a higher level than you, but you shouldn't expect them to do the hard work of figuring out how each individual experiment is related to the previous one. If you did A followed by B and then C, the order in which you present your results should reflect this, and make sure that the words you use to link them should help show how they're connected.

Let's look at an extract from a results section showing the end of one paragraph and the start of the next:

> ... As shown in Figure 3, an exposure lasting four hours was sufficient to trigger activation of the particle emitter.
> The beam strength was assessed by...

Box 2.1   Two paragraphs without connective language

This transition could be improved with the use of some linking phrases. Note how it's not just the extra words (italics) in the second paragraph of this next example that make the transition smoother, but that carrying over old information into the new paragraph (bold text) helps too:

> ... As shown in Figure 3, an exposure lasting four hours was sufficient to trigger activation of the **particle-emitter.**
>
> *In order to establish whether the* **emitted particle beam** *was sufficient to be of practical use,* the beam strength was assessed by...

Box 2.2   Two paragraphs connected with good signposting and flow

Level of detail

If you're following a set procedure in a lab with a known or expected outcome (which is common in the early years of a degree), you'll probably need to show the results of every step you carried out so your markers can check you're grasping these foundational elements. They will want to see evidence of how well you carried out the set procedure (in laboratory terms, the experimental 'protocol'). If something went wrong, then you can discuss the shortcomings in your discussion section.

If you had more control over the direction of the lab practical, the choice about which results to present will be yours. If you planned some experiments and they failed, you can usually omit these and dedicate the space to other experiments that worked. That's not to say you can pick and choose your favourite results: we simply mean that if an experiment failed for any reason such that its results are scientifically meaningless, there is no point in showing this to a marker if you have enough material to replace it with in your report.

Remember what we showed you in Figure 2.1 – most markers are primarily concerned with seeing that you can link results with theory, and are not interested in simply seeing a report of how well you did the experiments or how well you were able to learn a new skill. Your report shouldn't be a lab-book-style diary of your successes and failures. Failure, however, is not the same as having negative results. Negative results can be valuable and informative if you are confident you carried out a procedure properly – your controls should help you decide this – yet you still got an absence of any result. Perhaps this would even change the direction you take with subsequent experiments. This would be an appropriate scenario in which to write up negative findings.

Tone

The tone you take in your results section is particularly important. Your results section will probably contain the shortest, most direct sentences of your whole lab report. It's important to be unambiguous, and long sentences containing several concepts can lead you to confuse your reader rather than make things clearer for them. The use of pronouns (for example, 'they', 'it', 'them') can become confusing, particularly if the last time the object's proper name was mentioned is one or two sentences previously. Don't be afraid to be repetitive in your results section; it's far better here to be clear than to be stylish. You can find a deeper discussion on this aspect of your writing in Chapter 11 – Producing a Draft and Building your Argument.

There are conventions on how to use tenses. When you're reporting events that have taken place, your writing should be in the past tense:

- The reaction vessel was incubated at 65°C.
- The database was interrogated, and 25,000 records were identified.

When you present a result that was true at the time, is still true today, and will be true until someone shows otherwise, you should use the present simple tense.

- The optimum temperature for this reaction is 65°C.
- The database contains 25,000 relevant records.

Discussion

This is the accompaniment to your results section where you get to say everything about your data that you weren't allowed to before. You can think of it as the half where you *interpret*, as opposed to the previous half where you simply *show*. *Interpreting* in this context means doing things like talking about which results were surprising and which were expected, and what knowledge or logic makes you think this. You can point out parallels and contrasts between your findings and others published in the literature.

If you could think of your lab report as having an hourglass shape – narrow in the middle, and wide at the top (introduction) and bottom (conclusion) – you might see how the width of the hourglass relates to the width of your focus. In the introduction, you start off with a relatively wide-ranging discussion of context, background, and justification for the work. In the main body of the lab report you'll be looking at your own experiments in lots of minute detail. Here in your final discussion/conclusion section you have a chance to widen back out again, bringing the reader's attention back to the issues you raised at the start and showing how your findings have contributed to that academic discussion.

It's the section where you should mention any shortcomings in your experiments. This isn't for some nebulous reason of humility and admitting your mistakes: it's so that others reading your write-up can see *all* of the reasons that contributed to your findings.

To take the example we used earlier, perhaps you found that some varieties of plants survived the heat stress better than others. If, however, you later discovered that the rubber seal around the door of the oven door containing the resistant varieties was old and had dried out and cracked, you might reasonably doubt whether the hot air was properly contained. Maybe it was a small crack, unlikely to have had a huge impact on how much oven air mixed with the outside atmosphere in the room, but the seed of doubt is there, so you must write about it. If you were writing an article for publication and someone came along later and disproved your findings, you needn't worry about retracting your work because you alerted them to the fact there were potential inconsistencies in your materials. (Of course, as a professional scientist you'd have time to fix the issue and repeat the experiment, but as a student you probably won't have the luxury of doing it again.)

What most markers are concerned about, however, is whether you relate your findings to the theory you set out in the introduction. Remember that 75% of staff thought this was one of the primary benefits of lab reports. Here's what a connection between theory and results might look like in practice:

> In measurements of bacterial growth shown in Table 2, the number of bacteria present after six hours was significantly lower than anticipated. It is well-established that the time taken for *E. coli* to double is 20 to 30 minutes under optimal temperature and food conditions (Sezonov et al., 2007), so it must be concluded that the conditions in the incubator were not as programmed on the control panel. If this experiment were to be repeated, it would be advisable to feed a temperature probe into the cabinet to rest on top of the Petri dishes, so that the actual temperature of the dish could be monitored and checked in real time.

Box 2.3   Practical results connected with theory

This discussion excerpt not only reminds the reader of the finding (low growth rate), but it tells them precisely which table this detail came from. It then introduces a piece of theory which underpinned the experiment (standard rate of *E. coli* growth), cites the source of that knowledge, and mentions how this theory relates to the experiment. In this case, they relate by being contradictory. A good effort has been made to suggest improvements for the experimental protocol too, so this paragraph nicely exemplifies many things you should aim to do in your discussion section.

Variation on IMRaD: discussion and then conclusion, or conclusion and then discussion

Sometimes you may be asked to include a discussion as well as your conclusion. You might be asked to put them the other way around. The names given to each section don't matter, because there's only really one way to divide what is classically one section into two, and there's only one way round that this splitting makes sense.

Having this extra section doesn't generally mean much extra work. Unless you receive specific formatting instructions to the contrary, your job is just to separate everything you'd normally put in a discussion into these two separate parts.

In the first of the two, you should discuss the findings of *your own* work. Talk about the meaning of your data, and the shortcomings of your experimental procedures, and keep everything contained to a discussion about what you discovered yourself.

In the second of the two, relate your work to the wider theory of your field, and to other scientific works. Make recommendations about what should be done next (or what we should *stop* trying to do), or talk about what gain we now have a society as a result of gaining this new knowledge.

References

As with any piece of academic writing, you should include a list of your references in whichever style has been set by your course staff. You can read more about how to cite and reference in Chapter 8.

The Essay

Top 3 staff comments on essays:

▶ The student wrote about the concepts in a confusing, messy order so the essay is difficult to follow.

▶ The student didn't read the question properly so they've gone off-topic.

▶ This isn't written like an essay; it's just a report.

Top 3 student comments on essays:

▶ The science I'm writing about is quite straightforward, so I don't know how to make my essay stand out.

▶ I don't know what parts to put in an essay – can you show me a model answer so I know what you want?

▶ How can I express my opinion and still be objective?

As before with the lab report, the first thing we want to draw your attention to is the purpose and the audience.

Essays are used on science courses because they're the most well-established way of testing:

- your in-depth knowledge on a topic;
- your ability to communicate with a reader;
- your critical thinking skills;
- your ability to construct an argument.

We scientists don't generally think of ourselves as people who put forth arguments – why would we need to, when scientific facts should always represent the objective truth on their own, anyway? – but an argument is simply a statement supported by evidence. Scientists do this all the time. We make conclusions based on our findings. That involves interpreting the data, perhaps in light of other pieces of information from other places, and saying what it *tells us*.

Your purpose, then, is to demonstrate an ability to do these things to your marker.

Your literal audience will be your markers, but the audience you write for at university should always be *educated peers*. Educated in the sense that they have the same background knowledge that you have, but peers in the sense that they don't have any more knowledge than you. This means you should always fully explain things like abbreviations, acronyms, and new pieces of information you might have just discovered from current science reported in the media, or in peer-reviewed literature. Even though your lecturers would be able to understand these things too, they might simply not have read that same particular story or journal article, and so they may not be in a position to follow your meaning if you only give a brief mention. They are likely to be extremely busy running several modules for different year groups, and for students on completely different degrees, and many of them will also be leading research groups in labs. All of this means they probably have less time than they'd like to be able to keep up to date with every new development in their field. Therefore, you should aim to describe new developments in your essays as if to someone with a scientific education, but without prior knowledge of the specialism you're writing about.

Another way to think of this is to write to an audience of yourself at the beginning of your current year of study. If the information you're writing about was new to you this year, explain it in full. This shows your marker that you have a confident grasp of everything you're supposed to have been learning on their module.

Interpreting the question

Good essay questions will have up to three different parts. You'll find a command word or phrase which tells you what type of action to perform, there will be a statement of the topic, and there may also be a limiting part. Table 3.1 shows some examples.

Commands:	discuss, explain, list, compare and contrast (see Table 3.2 below for a longer list of command words and what they mean to a marker)
Subjects:	... veterinary treatments for farmed fish ... ... the methods available to quantify contamination of an aqueous solution with the CN^- ion ... ... the Davisson-Germer electron diffraction experiment ...
Limits:	... in elderly people. ... using only field equipment. ... and calculate the time a typical Z boson could stay in existence.

Table 3.1 Typical parts of a question

It's worth marking up your exam question paper in some way to prove to yourself you've identified each of these three different question parts, particularly if you're writing under exam conditions and are thus more time-pressured and more likely to feel stressed or rushed. A limiting part may not be present, or it may actually direct you to finish by widening the scope of your answer rather than narrowing it. Just don't forget it's there by the time you get two-thirds of the way through your essay and you're on a roll, writing everything you know about the subject.

Command words

These command words are commonly found in university assessments. Table 3.2 will give you an idea of what your markers are looking for when they use each one in their questions.

Command Word	Meaning
Analyse	Examine a process/theory in detail
Account for	Give an explanation of something, backed up with relevant evidence
Assess	To measure the value or importance of something
Compare	Point out similarities and differences between two processes/theories
Consider	Look closely at something
Contrast	Look at how two different things relate to each other, focusing on the differences
Critically analyse	Examine something in detail from an objective standpoint
Define	Give the exact meaning of
Demonstrate	Explain how something works/happens, with use of examples
Describe	Give a detailed account of a process/idea/thing
Detail	Describe a process/theory thoroughly, covering every possible point
Discuss	Talk about an idea/process in detail
Examine	Look at something in close detail
Evaluate	Give an assessment of the usefulness/importance/success of something
Formulate	Create a new idea/process
Interpret	Give an explanation for something based on the evidence
Justify	Provide evidence/reasoning to back up whatever statement is made in the question

Table 3.2   Common command words

Command Word	Meaning
Illustrate	Use examples/data/evidence to explain a concept or process
Outline	Give a description or explanation of something using only the main parts of the process/theory
Review	Give an overview of a theory/process
State	Say something clearly (often to give a definition or describe key stages in a process)
Summarise	Identify the key points and present these as concisely as possible

Table 3.2 *(Continued)*

Introductions

A very common piece of advice you may have been given in school is to rephrase the question in your introduction. We'd encourage you to go beyond this, as it's very simplistic and we don't often find this type of introduction attached to essays that achieve the highest grades. You should certainly tell the reader what's going to come later, but avoid phrases like 'In this essay I will ...' or 'This essay will compare and contrast ...'

Instead, try opening with a statement of a problem, or some other way of quickly making the case for why this essay topic is important, or at least show that you recognise why the markers thought it was worth asking about. As we said in the section about lab reports, it's also common to open an essay by saying that the topic is related to lowering costs, to increasing efficiency of procedures, to health benefits, or perhaps by convincing a reader that simply understanding whatever scientific principle you're going to discuss is a necessary step in understanding something more complex. Table 3.3 shows two versions of how an introduction might look.

The acceptable version of the introduction is minimally sufficient. It introduces the topic, which is good, but you should avoid opening your essay with a definition or a concept (bone weight) without first letting your reader become aware that this concept is coming. It promises to make a comparison, which is also good; if your reader knows what *type* of analysis is about to follow, they have one less thing to try to wrap their head around as they read on. However, this paragraph does a pretty bad job of setting up the topic. The author has almost got their structure entirely backwards, as they move from the specific issue (bone weight) to the more general ones (the fact that birds fly while mammals do not, and the fact that mammal and bird bones may be different in several ways).

Essay question	Compare and contrast the structures and functions of the bones of mammals with the bones of flying birds.
Acceptable opening strategy	Bird bones are lighter than mammal bones. Bones are important because they need to be strong, but also light to allow birds to fly. This essay will examine the differences between mammal and bird bone structures.
Much better opening strategy	Birds and mammals live by two very different lifestyle types – mammals are mainly ground-based, while most birds travel primarily through the air. This requires that bird bodies are physiologically adapted with a structure and composition that facilitates this mode of locomotion. This discussion will focus on one of these physiological adaptations: differences in bone composition.

Table 3.3 Opening essay sentences – a good and a better example

The improved version of this introduction first establishes the reason for making the comparison. To generalise from this example, the first two sentences tell the reader 'These two things (birds and mammals) are different (flying vs not flying). If we can understand what is different about them (physiology), we can begin to understand *how* these different structures are useful in carrying out their distinct functions'. The better example is also related directly back to the question. It also goes from a broad statement to a narrow one, helping us to anticipate what is about to come next in the main body of the essay.

The main body

Setting out the basics

The command words in the question will tell you to do something specific, but before you can do anything complex, you first need to arm your reader with the essential knowledge they will need later. You can think of this as the 'exposition' stage, where you 'expose' the necessary facts. If, for example, you're going to discuss the use of a particular set of techniques that can all serve the same purpose, it would be premature to jump immediately into comparing them. You may need to mention what each technique involves, perhaps why it is used, and by whom, and in which scenarios. By telling the reader these factors are involved, they will be in a much better position to understand your comparison later.

If you're very early in your degree, your command words might only direct you to do something very simple and linear (describe, explain, list), and this is probably to let your markers check you've learned the facts of your subject. Once you move beyond this stage and your markers start asking you to do more complex things (discuss, evaluate, justify), you'll need to think about what each of those commands mean, and how to fulfil them.

Structuring your paragraphs

A well-planned essay will always achieve better marks than one that was written as the author went along. You will either have a limited word count or limited time, so planning allows you first think about which points you'd like to make, and then to decide which you've got the space or the time to discuss. If you do this before you put pen to paper (or fingers to keyboard), you'll avoid the familiar scenario of using asterisks and arrows to insert extra information you only thought of right at the end, or running out of time before you've discussed everything.

At this point, look back to our list of command words and think about what particular type of task you have to carry out in your assignment.

Each paragraph should be about one point. You should open with a topic sentence, develop upon that topic, and perhaps conclude or signpost to the reader that a new topic is coming next.

You could develop a paragraph by detail:

> The largest blood vessel in the body is the aorta. It emerges from the left ventricle of the heart and is the first conduit for all of the oxygenated blood destined for the rest of the body. It must deal with a huge amount of pressure, so it has thick, elastic walls and a large internal diameter. The aorta extends a short distance above the heart, turns at the aortic arch (where several arteries branch off to deliver blood to the head and arms), and descends through the abdomen to supply blood to the lower body.

... by chronology:

> Viral infection involves several steps. First, a part of the viral coat must come into physical contact with a cell from the host organism. Second, a specific interaction between a protein on the viral coat and a matching protein on the host cell surface occurs, allowing the virus to 'dock'. If the host cell does not have the appropriate protein, infection will not occur (at least, not at that cell type; this is why cold and flu infection only happens in the lungs, for example). Third, the virus injects its genetic material into the host cell. Fourth, the host cell's transcription and translation machinery takes the genetic material and carries out the instructions, thereby creating new copies of the virus. Finally, the virus must emerge from the host cell, either by budding out or by rupturing the cell membrane.

... or by example:

> There are many different structures a crystal can take. The most basic is the simple cubic cell, which consists of equally spaced rows and columns of atoms arranged in a simple grid structure. More complex is the simple cubic lattice; if one cube of 8 atoms at the vertices were to be viewed in isolation, it would feature one extra atom at the centre of the cube, for a total of 9. More complex again is the face-centred cubic lattice. This is similar to the simple cubic lattice, but with an atom at the centre of each of its 6 *faces* rather than just one at the centre of the cube, for a total of 14 atoms per unit.

Note that the first example also included a signpost sentence at the end.

> The aorta extends a short distance above the heart, turns at the aortic arch (where several arteries branch off to deliver blood to the head and arms), and descends through the abdomen to supply blood to the lower body.

The hypothetical paragraph that would follow this could be about the circulation in the head and arms, or it could be about the circulation in the lower body; either way, we've been primed to expect it. Signpost-style conclusions or transitions are not necessary for every paragraph, but they can help the reader anticipate what's about to come next, thereby smoothing their progression through your essay.

If you can make your writing easier to follow, then you'll have demonstrated good communication skills and you'll be more likely to attain a higher mark. Look at pp. 145–150 for more examples of how to build paragraphs from sentences, and see Chapter 11 – Producing a Draft and Building Your Argument more generally for a more in-depth discussion of how planning and paragraphing will help you make the best of your writing.

Concluding

The classical advice about conclusions is to relate your discussion back to the question you were set. Much like we said in our section on introductions, we'd strongly encourage you to go beyond clichéd phrases like 'In this essay I have compared and contrasted ...' or 'This piece has evaluated X and Y, and I would recommend ...' It doesn't take much to be more sophisticated. Table 3.4 shows two examples.

Question	Using the parameters provided, estimate the suitability of these different hydrodynamic system designs for delivering liquids to their destinations.
Acceptable closing strategy	In this assignment I have shown the different forces imparted by different pipe materials, in order to evaluate whether the materials were suitable for water transport systems. The best surface to use was plastic with no surface texture. I would therefore recommend that this design was used in the future.
Much better closing strategy	Of the six materials evaluated here for suitability for use as pipe-lining material, a plastic interior surface with a medium bore and without any texture provided the lowest resistance to the passing fluid. By applying the relevant theoretical physical principles, it has been shown that this material created the least friction and this diameter was not so narrow as to induce drag, but not so wide as to cause a drop in hydrodynamic pressure. Further investigations into the use of grooves and fins to direct the fluid flow may reveal even more efficient designs, particularly at intersections of pipe segments where the direction of flow needs to change.

Table 3.4   Closing essay sentences – a good and a better example

In the better example:

- we're reminded immediately what the essay question was about;
- we're reminded what method was used;
- the best option is highlighted again;
- the complexity of the issue is acknowledged with a mention about alternative scenarios.

Note how the writer carefully picks out the most relevant pieces of information that must have come from various different paragraphs of the body of the assignment. The writer also manages to make a conclusion without ever referring to him- or herself. Instead of saying '*I would therefore recommend...*'you could say '*the evidence presented here* supports the conclusion that...'.

Your marker will be interested in seeing whether you can select the most relevant parts of your essay to form this reminder section at the end. You will have spent a long time thinking deeply about the essay, but try to imagine how a marker will approach it. They'll probably have only a few minutes to spend reading a couple of thousand words from each person in your class, so they don't have the same luxury you had of being able to turn things over in their mind and consider them deeply. Treat them kindly by making your points clearly, with appropriately short sentences, separated into new paragraphs for each subtopic, and then finish by reminding them what they've just heard.

If you only remember one thing about essay writing for the rest of your university career, remember this:

First, tell your reader what you're about to tell them.
Next, tell them it.
Finally, tell them what you just told them.

Worked example

One very common temptation for us as scientists is to tell our readers the facts we know in a linear order. This is commendable, and generally *is* the best way to do things, but you might want to alter this approach when thinking about the large-scale structure of an essay.

Imagine you had to write an essay on this question:

Compare and contrast the various methods used to treat obesity in European healthcare systems.

There are several things we can predict about the structure of this essay immediately: there should be more than one method discussed, as an in-depth explanation of what you believe to be the single best approach is not what the question asks for; the methods should be directly compared to each other, as it is not enough to explain them separately and expect the reader to notice how they are similar and how they differ; only methods common to European healthcare systems should be discussed; and that you should probably include some level of analysis and recommendation in your conclusions. Being at university challenges you to apply and use your knowledge, not just prove that you can recall it.

Now, how might your research on this topic be categorised?

If you have been sensible with your literature search, you will have started with review articles (if this term doesn't mean anything to you, have a look at Chapter 7 – Researching the Topic and Evaluating Your Materials and Chapter 10 – Being Critical). These review articles will have been written by very experienced people in the field of public health and nutrition, and they will have summarised (or 'reviewed') the last several years' worth of research on obesity. Such wide-ranging articles as reviews will usually have a substantial introduction explaining what causes obesity, how much of a problem it is, and why we need to prevent it. Reviews are a rich source of references to other primary research articles which allow you to a) get more detail and depth on your knowledge, and b) check the validity and truth of what's reported in the review.

It's very tempting to immerse yourself in reading background-type articles like this, but bear in mind that your time is finite, and that your essay question doesn't ask anything about the causes of obesity, its prevalence, or its economic impact. Don't dwell on interesting surface-level topics like these; move on to reading about the details of the treatments used.

It's important that you apply the principles from Chapter 9 to your search technique in order to make your job faster and easier. Most literature databases will allow you to sort your results by date (reverse chronological order is usually the default setting – note that this is different from everyday search engines, whose algorithms make assumptions about what kind of results you're most interested in and put those at the top. This means it's completely inappropriate to think that the top results from a scientific database are always going to be the 'best' ones for your search term). In this case, it's true that treatments generally improve with time. Perhaps this means you will download some articles and categorise them by timeframe: 5–10 years ago, 2–5 years ago, and the last year. This might be an appropriate system depending on your essay question, but in our particular case it's not the best. Things might have been different if the question had said 'Give an account of the development of modern treatments for obesity and compare their effectiveness', but it does not.

This is an important point, as markers in the sciences often complain that their students' essays are written with this chronological structure. It's not bad, but it doesn't allow us to see whether you've understood the topic at a deeper level. A historical account like we've just described is called a narrative structure, based around a storyline. A narrative is sometimes appropriate, but it's too simplistic for this 'compare and contrast' type question.

Instead, you might want to categorise the articles on the basis of what is found inside.

Public health workers, like nurses, sometimes visit schools and talk to children about healthy eating. They might teach them about: the significance of dietary sugar and fat; the classical food groups; the importance of exercise in the balance of energy taken in with energy expended; and about portion control. You might read articles on all of these types of intervention and categorise them with those same four headings.

It is also common for health workers to talk to families in their communities about nutrition. This work might involve explaining to parents how they could serve as role models for good eating habits, or giving advice on preparing meals that everyone can eat together so as to more closely monitor and guide the children's nutrition. You might do some reading on this and decide these articles fall under the categories of 'cooking', 'meal times', and 'budget'.

Then you might find articles about interventions that occur after a child has become dangerously obese. These could include reports about new surgical methods, new drugs given to reduce fat absorption from food, or combinations of these. These could be categorised as articles about 'surgical treatment' and 'pharmacological treatment'.

Any of these categorisations would be appropriate, and you might think of others, too. The point of categorising the articles you read is to help you break away from writing a historical narrative and instead think about grouping things sensibly.

A structure based on the categories you identified in your research phase is far easier for a marker to read. We'll give a worked example of how to use reading and research to inform that plan here.

Returning one more time to our essay question, let's analyse the wording piece by piece.

Compare and contrast the various methods used to treat obesity in European healthcare systems.

This has a typical three-part structure: command, subject, and limits. The command here is to 'compare and contrast'. The subject is treatment methods for obesity. The limit is to stick to methods from Europe. (A limit won't always be present, and sometimes it may actually direct you to expand the scope, but the important point is that you don't forget about it in the excitement of writing everything you know about the subject.)

Table 3.5 shows a possible structure based on categories we mentioned.

Intro	What is obesity? Define
	Why is it a problem?
	• Economics – hospitals cost money
	• Health – life quality and length are affected
	• Society and governance – people are out of work – welfare payments
	How does Europe differ from other places?
	• Can you think of unifying features?
	• Do healthcare systems in different parts of Europe actually deal with things in very different ways, and what are those?
	• Do countries across Europe face the same levels of obesity?
Solutions	Sugar and fat awareness in schools
	Exercise advice
	Cooking lessons
	Meal timing advice
	Budget modelling for families

Table 3.5   One possible structural plan for this essay

	Surgery – case studies on new treatments
	Surgery – large trials on old, established treatments
	Drugs – case studies on new treatments
	Drugs – large trials on old, established treatments
Discussion	Remind reader which types of treatment worked very well vs not at all
	Remind reader which treatment methods only worked in certain parts of Europe
	Make a case for which consideration is most important (low cost? high effectiveness?)
	Use this to justify which treatment you think is best, and would recommend

Table 3.5   *(Continued)*

This is certainly better than a historical narrative that describes how we came to today's treatment methods, and it certainly breaks things down into a fine enough level of detail that you could begin writing an essay from it. Depending on the length of your essay, you might find this a bit much to fit in. In that case, it becomes important to make decisions about what to omit.

Whittling everything down to a manageable amount for your essay/ dissertation

We've already alluded to the fact that you'll be able to read far more than you could ever write about. Even after you think you've found a suitable number of articles to read, you'll probably find you can't write about them all. Don't become a purely strategic essay-writer, determined to win the game of fitting all of your reading into your work. You'll be rewarded more for producing a high-quality, clear, well-structured essay that flows well with a reasoned argument than you will for demonstrating how many articles you downloaded.

Building a plan like the one outlined above is the strongest piece of advice we can give you to help you decide what to include and what to omit. Every discipline is different, as is every essay question, so there's no rule-of-thumb answer we can give. We can, however, give you some questions to ask yourself that might help you make that decision:

1 How many words do I have left to use within my word limit?
2 How many words will it realistically take to adequately describe the most important points I've found in each of these articles?

3 What command have I been given? (If it's a comparison-type, you'll need to allocate more of your word count to highlighting the ways things are similar to or differ from each other.)

4 What type of essay would be best – a comparison between the most opposite methods, which could produce a lot of discussion, or a comparison between the most similar and most effective methods, which could give you the chance to discuss the pros and cons of very small details?

5 Can any of these articles be grouped?

If you have limited space within your word count, perhaps the best way to condense your reading is to think in terms of larger themes. For example, the plan mentioned above could be reduced to something more like the outline in Table 3.6.

Intro	What is obesity? Define
	Why is it a problem? • Economics – hospitals cost money • Health – life quality and length are affected • Society and governance – people are out of work – welfare payments
	How does Europe differ from other places? • Can you think of unifying features? • Do healthcare systems in different parts of Europe actually deal with things in very different ways, and what are those? • Do countries across Europe face the same levels of obesity?
Solutions	School-based advice
	Home and family-based advice
	Medical interventions
Discussion	Remind reader which types of treatment worked very well vs not at all
	Remind reader which treatment methods only worked in certain parts of Europe
	Make a case for which consideration is most important (low cost? high effectiveness?)
	Use this to justify which treatment you think is best, and would recommend

Table 3.6   A revised, more focused essay plan

You would need to work hard to avoid the temptation of still writing about each of the studies you'd researched anyway. To avoid that, you might want to take these three broad themes and give them a paragraph or two each, instead of writing one paragraph about each article. You could say, for example, what school-based advice usually involves, and mention a couple of studies that worked. You could then take a second paragraph to mention some studies that had no effect. In each of these paragraphs, you could highlight the reasons why you think they were or were not successful. This fulfils part of the requirement to compare and contrast as you go, as you'll have a chance to point out why some school-based interventions worked and some didn't.

Revising your plan as you go

The last thing we want to say about the planning and research phase of writing an essay is that you shouldn't be afraid to alter your plans in light of new things you read, or new decisions you make as you write. If you have flexibility to choose your own essay or dissertation topic, you will most likely change your mind more than once about what to focus on. The reading and research process will probably be daunting, possibly frustrating, and definitely not a simple, linear process.

For this reason, we'd advise that you don't begin to write your introduction until you've got the rest of the text mostly complete. You might decide to drop a whole branch of your reading because you find that you don't have space in your word count. Incorporating too many small pieces of information on related topics is usually not as good as writing well about just a few. If you're worried about seeming like you've missed big, obvious topics out, you might find you can tell your marker that those subtopics exist in your introduction, and explain why you've chosen not to examine them in detail. A signpost like this towards the end of an introduction might suit our European obesity example:

There have been many school-based interventions across Europe designed to teach children about the importance of dietary sugar and fat, of exercise, of the classical food groups, and about controlling the size of portions they take. For reasons of brevity, in this discussion they will collectively be referred to as 'school-based interventions', and notably successful examples will be discussed in more detail.

The Dissertation

Top 3 staff comments on dissertations:

▶ There's lots of minute and unnecessary detail about published experiments.
▶ It seems to be a big descriptive literature review without a selective focus on any particular aspect.
▶ I don't know what conclusion the student reached or how well they've understood and interpreted everything they've read.

Top 3 student comments on dissertations:

▶ What purpose is a dissertation supposed to serve?
▶ How do I know when to stop reading and start writing?
▶ What types of section does a dissertation need to have?

A dissertation is probably the longest piece of written work you'll produce in your degree. Depending on the requirements of your particular degree, it might take the form of an extended practical lab report or a literature-based research project. In either case, it will test your ability to come up with a research question, decide on an appropriate strategy to get some answers, and document the process and the findings at a depth you probably won't have gone to before.

Sometimes a student is paired with a research supervisor who already has a dissertation project in mind. It's common in science for supervisors to want to find out which of these projects are likely to yield interesting results, but they don't want to bring in a PhD student or a postdoctoral researcher for a long commitment without first testing the waters. It may also be that a supervisor has a rough idea about a brand new long-term project, but hasn't had the time to properly assess the current literature on the topic enough to decide how to proceed. In both cases, honours and master's dissertation projects are an ideal way for research groups to run 'pilot' studies while training up new students such as you.

To reflect this reality, we'll split the following sections into two parts, as some of the advice for a lab-based dissertation won't apply to literature research projects, and vice versa.

If you're writing a dissertation for a master's degree, the same advice will apply but your word count will be higher. The biggest ramification of this is that you will probably have multiple chapters, but the rest of our advice is broadly applicable. As always, take a steer from your course coordinators on the magnitude of the project ahead of you as they'll be the ones marking it.

The document itself

A dissertation should have very clear boundaries between different sections, similarly to the way parts of a lab report are clearly delineated. Both lab-based and literature-based dissertations should open with an introduction that explains the rationale for your research, and thereafter the styles will start to diverge.

Lab-based dissertation	Library project
Title page	
Declaration of originality	
Abstract	
Acknowledgements	
Table of contents	
List of figures	
List of tables	
List of abbreviations	
Introduction – literature review	Introduction – justification for research
Materials and methods	Methods
Chapter 1: Results	Chapter 1
Chapter 1: Discussion	
Chapter 2: Results	Chapter 2
Chapter 2: Discussion	
Chapter 3: Results	Chapter 3
Chapter 3: Discussion	
General discussion	
Appendices (if required)	
References	

Table 4.1 Typical sections of a dissertation

What we've called chapters here don't necessarily need to be called chapters, especially if you're doing a project with one central theme that builds in a linear way rather than branching out into subthemes. Rather than numbering them as Chapter 1, Chapter 2 and so on, you might instead give these sections descriptive headings that signpost what's contained within, for example '1. Nanofabrication Methods', '2. Applications of Nanofabrication', '3. Assessment of a Novel Nanofabrication Technique'. You don't need to have three of these, but a good, substantial dissertation might have two or three different subtopics. Giving these clearly delineated sections is a way of helping the reader make sense of the huge amount of information you're going to present, so don't feel that using chapters is a way of cheating on your structure.

Introduction

This is where you explain the need for your dissertation project, and tell us about the information we already have on the topic. Is there a gap in our knowledge? Is there a problem you hope to solve? Convince your reader why your project is necessary. You might like to imagine that your reader will decide whether or not to fund your research. What would persuade them?

Your supervisor will be able to help you with formulation of a research question and/or a hypothesis (these are subtly different things), and a methodology. If you're working on a lab-based dissertation, it may be that all of these three things have already been decided by them.

Lab-based: You should spend most of your introduction creating a literature review. This is important because you need to show us that your own lab work is based on a solid foundation of existing conclusions so that we are clear about why you've chosen to begin your series of experiments in the way that you have.

Literature-based: Most of the rest of your dissertation will take the form of an extended literature review, so you can afford to be more brief and concise with your introduction. Don't try to analyse too much literature here yet; simply justify the need for your research.

As with a lab report, end your introduction with a statement of your aims and objectives. Budget around 10% of your word count – perhaps less if your dissertation is literature-based, as your whole dissertation is essentially a literature review and thus you don't need to cover so much literature in your introduction –

but adjust upwards or downwards if your supervisor agrees that you have a sensible reason to do so. Your dissertation supervisor will help you determine how many sources to draw upon and cite, given the norms in your discipline.

End your introduction by restating your aims, objectives, hypothesis, or research question.

Materials and methods

In either type of dissertation, you'll need to tell your reader something about *how* you did what you did.

Lab-based: This should take the usual format that you'll be familiar with from writing lab reports. If you have a large number of methods spanning several pages, you can think about splitting them into categories with different descriptive headings, such as 'gene cloning methods' and 'tissue culture methods'. It makes most sense to group methods according to their purpose, rather than alphabetically, for example, so that a reader who is interested in an experiment that lasts a whole week and involves several steps will be able to follow the whole methodology in a coherent sequence without flipping back and forth.

Always explain your methods in full, as you would find in a published scientific article. Markers tend to disapprove of methods that say things like '... was carried out according to the manufacturer's instructions', or '... was mixed according to established procedure'. You need to demonstrate that you are aware of those instructions. At a viva (formally a *viva voce*, Latin for 'living voice' – an oral examination which often accompanies a dissertation project) – you may be asked to explain why those steps were carried out. This part of the exam ensures you were not blindly following instructions without an understanding of what each step was actually for, so learn this early and write each method out in full.

Literature-based: Since your research is based on published literature, your marker will want to know how you found it. Some disciplines may demand a very specific way of detailing your search strategy, while others will accept a looser descriptive account. Perhaps the most rigorous guideline is PRISMA (**P**referred **R**eporting **I**tems for **S**ystematic reviews and **M**eta-**A**nalyses) (Liberati et al., 2009; Moher et al., 2009) which you will easily find a description of online. This system has developed since the 1990s as a way for researchers writing systematic reviews in medicine to be clear and precise about how they chose the papers they decided to write about. A 'PRISMA-compliant' methods section would detail things like the search terms you used when searching your literature database, the number of results you got, the number of articles you rejected as being irrelevant to the scope of your research question, and then the process you went through in analysing each paper. PRISMA is specifically designed for researchers carrying out systematic reviews and meta-analyses, but even if you're not going to such rigorous lengths in your library project, you might think about adopting some of these best-practice principles in your methods section.

Chapters

Chapters are useful if you have different strands to your research. They make things easier for your reader to digest. If you're using chapters, you'll need to decide whether to include a discussion segment in each chapter, or whether to leave the bulk of your discussion until the end of the whole dissertation. The greater the differences between your chapters, the greater the need for a chapter-by-chapter discussion, as a set of quite unrelated results would be difficult to integrate in one long discussion at the end.

Lab-based: Perhaps your project was a completely new one for the people in the lab where you were based, and this meant you had little or nothing to build upon, so you ended up trying a few different things at the same time. This kind of 'portfolio' project is ideally suited to a write-up in different chapters. Another reason for chaptering might be that you were testing out two very different methodologies to try to achieve the same outcome because no-one had ever attempted anything like it before, so you were evaluating one relative to the other. If there were very different outcomes for each method, equally rich in learning points, your reader will probably find it easier to read about them separately. A third common reason for using chapters is that a project was very successful and proceeded very quickly, in which case you'd end up with lots of data garnered from successive experiments. If you can identify natural points at which to break these findings into distinct 'stories', each with an aim, an investigation phase, and a result, then your chapter structure would follow these delineations.

Literature-based: The same principles as above regarding whether to break into chapters will apply, but your presentation and your discussion of the literature should be much more closely integrated. This means you won't have a need for separate results and discussion sections. Chapter 11 – Producing a Draft and Building Your Argument will show you how to use your reading to formulate your thoughts into a coherent argument and then structure this appropriately into paragraphs and sections.

You will need to consider how your reader will deal with all this new information. Think carefully about which facts need to come first; lay out the basics of your field before you progress to complex analyses; and remember that your audience for any university work should be educated peers, so don't write with someone who is already a subject expert in mind. Your marker needs to see evidence that you have a good understanding of everything you're saying, so you can't afford to take shortcuts.

Review articles will make good models of how to carry out a dissertation. Find a couple of fairly long review articles in your field (tens of pages) and dedicate some time to reading them with an eye to their structure. Look at how much information the author(s) give in the introduction vs how much they leave until the main body of the article. Next, look at how many headed sections they have. Can you see a logic to the way they've divided these up? Are they dividing by major topic? Are they dividing by the type of analysis they're performing? Look at whether they do any sort of discussion or conclusion in each section before moving on to the next, or whether this is done in a separate section at the end. Pay attention to the language they use for this. You might be able to incorporate some of those useful phrases into your own writing to make it more professional.

Your ability to critically analyse literature plays a major role in determining how well you score in a dissertation; see Chapter 10 – Being Critical for more on this.

General discussion

Your supervisor will be the best-placed person to advise on the balance between your chapter-by-chapter discussions and this general discussion at the end. You will certainly need one main final conclusion, as, regardless of how extensive your chapter-by-chapter discussion sections are, you'll still need to tie up the scientific discussion you opened in your introduction. It should serve exactly the same function as a conclusion to an essay: it's your chance to remind your reader of the highlights of your findings and to relate them back to the wider theoretical concepts you introduced at the start, or to demonstrate the real-world applicability of what you've shown.

Appendices

These are usually required only if you have large data sets, or if you have carried out any statistical analyses and you think it would add value for your reader to show the detailed tables of results from those tests. An appendix is a place to put data for reference only, so it shouldn't include any discussion or interpretation. Readers will only turn to an appendix if directed to do so in the main body of the text, after which they will turn straight back to the main body, so don't spend time making this section beautifully written. It should be a simple, functional addition to your dissertation. Each individual dataset should be presented in a different appendix / numbered subsection within your appendix. This makes it easy for your reader to turn to the right page quickly. For the same reason, your table of contents should also include a line for each appendix or each subsection.

References

As with any piece of academic work, your list of referenced materials should come at the end. The choice of format (Harvard, Vancouver, APA etc) may be up to you and you should check with your university before you begin so that you don't need to spend time reformatting this later. Organising your references will probably be the second most time-consuming of all of your dissertation tasks – the first of which will probably be ensuring that your data is properly displayed (Chapter 9 – Working with Data), and that the whole dissertation is properly formatted page-by-page, so be sure to leave plenty of time for referencing.

You need to check that your in-text citations are all correct, and in the right place within each sentence or paragraph. You also need to check that you reference list meets the criteria set by your markers. If they don't specify exactly which style to use, pick one and stick to it. Consistency throughout your dissertation is far more important to your reader than your choice of whether to put the title or the author's name in capitals, for example. See Chapter 8 for more detail on how to use other people's work.

The Poster

Top 3 staff comments on posters:

► The best posters contain a lot less text than you might expect.
► Standing by my poster at a conference is the easiest way to network.
► I make up my mind about whether to read a poster or walk past in about five seconds.

Top 3 student comments on posters:

► Aren't posters a little childish?
► How many columns should they have, and at what font size?
► I'm not sure how to make this different from an essay printed on a poster-sized piece of paper.

Posters are an unusual beast. Very few people outside of the advertising and merchandising industry use posters to try to communicate with an audience, so creating one for a non-commercial purpose can be a challenge for a student until it's clear what its job is to be.

Posters are designed to be read by a standing or walking audience, displayed as part of a larger collection. This means that part of your poster's job is to make someone stop and read. As a student, you'll be asked to make posters to show you can balance the requirement to communicate your knowledge or data against the skill of being concise. The audience won't begin to read if there's too much text to get through in a couple of minutes. You need to become proficient in identifying your major points, convincing the reader why they're worth reading about (i.e. opening with a strong introduction), and perhaps supporting all of this with images, figures, or graphs. Visuals should attract a walking audience member, and should help you convey a lot of information without resorting to long blocks of text.

If you go into a career in academia, you'll have to create posters to take to conferences. If not, posters created for your degree will probably be displayed in a similar setup, for example, in an open space for people to walk around. Conferences are opportunities for researchers to get together and listen to a small number of presentations from selected experts over the course of a few days, and to meet other researchers who may be working on similar topics and share notes or set up collaborations. A poster acts like a quick advert for a scientist and their research, and they're usually displayed at specific networking sessions during the course of a conference where everyone is free to walk through the display hall and speak with the authors while they're stood next to their posters.

The format and layout

Posters are typically printed at A0 or A1 size. This perhaps gives you more space than you've ever used for a single-page document before, but don't forget that it has to be read from a distance of a few feet. As an exercise, print a page of text and put it on your wall. Stand back far enough that you would comfortably be able to see a whole A0 sheet of paper from that distance, and ask yourself if the font needs to be larger. Usually, on a first attempt, the answer is 'yes'.

The human eye isn't accustomed to reading long horizontal pieces of text. This is perhaps one reason that books are usually presented in portrait layout, and why newspaper articles (and scientific ones!) are presented in columns. Your poster will need to be split into columns too, unless you've opted for an unusual layout to reflect an unusual idea that may be best represented in a non-linear way. These columns should read from top to bottom, and progress from the left edge of the poster to the right.

You may want to go further with the visual organisation and give each section its own box, still arranged in columns like a scientific article. Of course, you'll need headings on the sections, but anything you can do to subtly help the potential reader orient themselves with the content will make them a little more likely to stop and read your poster.

Remember to include a small reference section at the end. You are unlikely to use lots of references, particularly if your poster relates mainly to some work that you carried out yourself, but it's still crucial that you cite your sources appropriately. Make sure that you also give named credit to anyone who contributed to the poster in a by-line below the title, and to acknowledge any funding bodies who supplied money for you to be able to carry out the work. This is typically done by incorporating their name or their logo into a small section of acknowledgements.

Attracting your audience

A good poster should be at the same time eye-catching and professional. Bright colours are sure to catch the eye, but would you really trust the scientific findings of someone who worked in neon colours and added gratuitous decorations? We've certainly seen some well-made interactive posters where the audience were able to, for example, pull various tabs to change the images visible through cut-out windows on the poster to illustrate the different stages of a molecular process. These embellishments were added for a sound educational reason, though, so be cautious with your enthusiasm. You are expected to make your posters professional, which means paying attention to the font, the colours, the layout, the images, and the language you choose to use.

Images and figures

We want you to feel encouraged to make liberal use of these in your posters. The average viewer will be willing to dedicate only a few seconds to deciding whether they should stop and read your poster or move on to the next one. Images and figures give them something easy and intuitive to look at, they reduce the number of words your audience must read, and they give you something engaging to discuss if an audience member decides to approach you and ask questions.

The Abstract

Top 3 staff comments on abstracts:

▶ Students dive right into the details of their experiment without explaining the rationale or theory behind the work.

▶ This section should make someone want to read more, so it needs to be concise as well as conveying the impact of the findings.

▶ Don't just describe what the reader will find in the rest of the piece; tell them the interesting information now.

Top 3 student comments on abstracts:

▶ How long does an abstract have to be?

▶ How much detail should I go into?

▶ Should I tell my reader what my results are, or leave that for the main body?

Even though they're usually very short pieces of writing (200–300 words), we've given abstracts their own section here because they're a very common academic format. Although they can be attached to several different types of longer pieces, the format is always the same.

The purpose

An abstract is a short piece of summary text found at the start of a longer piece of work, such as a scientific article, lab report, or in a conference programme to advertise each presentation. Its job is to relay the main points of the main piece in such a way as to make any potential readers take notice and decide to read on. You'll find one at the start of every peer-reviewed scientific article. This is necessary for the survival of journals because the publishers rely on readers paying a subscription to read the articles. If potential readers didn't have access to the abstracts, they'd only be able to see the article titles and the names of the authors, making it highly unlikely that any readers would ever pay to download an article. (As a student, your university library will almost always pay for your access to articles. In Chapter 7 – Researching the Topic and Evaluating Your Materials, we'll explain how your library may have a budget to pay for articles published in journals that they don't subscribe to. If you ever come across an article like this, but the abstract makes it sound particularly useful, showing the abstract to your course coordinator or librarian may help convince them why they should pay for it on your behalf.) This means the abstract should advertise the science to the reader: it should want to make them know more.

As a student, you'll potentially need to write one at the start of some of the longer lab reports in your degree. You might not be asked to do this in first year, but you almost certainly will by the time you get to your final year project. Master's theses and PhD theses need abstracts too, so if you plan to go on to have a career in academia, you'll need to become familiar with how to create a good one.

The good news is that the abstract should only contain information found in the rest of the piece that follows, so you simply need to identify a few key parts of your story and package them up in this one summary paragraph. It also means you should never make any claims that aren't supported by the text.

The content

You can think of an abstract as answers to the most important standard questions a reader might have:

- What did the researcher(s) want to know?
- How did they go about finding out the answer?
- What did they find?
- What does this mean for us now?

These questions should be answered within a few hundred words. When double-spaced, it would certainly be unusual to find an abstract stretching to more than a single side of A4.

So how do you make your science seem appealing? We're not suggesting that you should inflate your results to make them seem more impactful than they really are. The data are the data, and a negative answer is as scientifically interesting as a positive one. Rather, think about the real-world significance of your work. What was the gap in our knowledge that meant the project was worth carrying out? Tell your reader so they can appreciate the context.

When it comes to describing the methods in your abstract, the reader doesn't need to know every technique you used. Instead of focusing on the *methods*, consider describing the *methodology*. The word *methodology* relates to the *broad type* of approach you took. For example, '*Using postal questionnaires*, the perceived effectiveness of home-based nursing care vs hospital care of elderly patients was evaluated' or 'This investigation looked at the excitation and ionisation of various isotopes *using femtosecond laser radiation delivered across a range of wavelengths*'. The details of which methods were actually used should go into the Methods section in the main body of the piece.

You can summarise your results very briefly in an abstract. Your reader is probably only interested in the one main finding – the maximum value, or the optimum value, or whatever else is absolutely key in your specific research.

Finally, the question of 'What does this mean for us now?' is subtly different from 'What did the researcher(s) want to know?' as the former deals with generalities and the latter with specifics. If surveys suggested that patients were unhappy with their home-based nursing care, perhaps the recommendation at the end of the abstract (and, by definition, the end of the report itself) should be to reduce the healthcare system's reliance on home-based nursing, or to address the reasons for this perception. If the laser experiment deepened our understanding of quantum behaviour, perhaps this would open the path for new experiments we had never conceived of before. Forward-looking statements such as these make good endings to abstracts.

Common errors

An abstract should never contain information not found in the body of your research. It's important, too, that you don't twist your findings or augment your data to make it sound 'sexier'. A study published in the Journal of the American Medical Association (JAMA) looked at a sample of peer-reviewed articles and counted the percentage of abstracts containing errors or miscommunications about the content contained in the articles themselves, and found a surprisingly high frequency (Pitkin et al., 1999). Another study featuring the same lead author assessed whether it was effective to intervene during the peer-review stages by adding a cover note to the articles' authors explaining the nature of any deficiencies uncovered in their abstracts (Pitkin and Branagan, 1998). The intervention was alarmingly ineffective. If you are interested, read these two articles. You will gain some insight into the types of errors it's possible to make, and perhaps this knowledge will stop you from making the same mistakes yourself. (Note: Ironically, you'll notice that the structure of the abstracts of these two articles are slightly different from what we've just described. JAMA has an in-house style which dictates that every article's abstract follows a very strict pattern, complete with standard headings. This is an exception rather than the rule, so don't be confused when you encounter it.)

Preparing to Write

Researching the Topic and Evaluating Your Materials

Top 3 staff comments on finding materials:

▶ Some sources aren't academic enough.
▶ Some students use academic databases the same way they use search engines, which means they trust what they're shown at first and don't know how to find the most important sources.
▶ Source material often isn't woven together into a new structure very well.

Top 3 student comments on finding materials:

▶ How many sources is enough before I start writing?
▶ Is Google Scholar useful at university? Where should I be searching?
▶ What type of sources do I need to read?

The most daunting part of a written assignment is often knowing how to get started. What should you do first? Where should you go to find information? How do you even know what information to try to find? Usually you'll need to base your work on something someone else has said previously. Whether you're writing an essay, a lab report, or a large dissertation, you need to convince your reader that what you'll say is based on solid science. To do that, you need to walk them through the key parts of what that science is. To do *that*, you'll need to make sure you've found it and interpreted it appropriately.

'Gathering materials' also describes the process of choosing what to present from a collection of results you've generated yourself. We'll cover that towards the end of this chapter in the section about Evaluating and Refining Your Materials on p. 62.

Throughout this chapter, we'll describe how to quickly find relevant information from:

- books
- scientific journal articles

and we'll move on to discuss how to evaluate each of these source types, as well as:

- internet sources
- your own experimental findings.

Books

Uses

Books are used routinely in the early stages of an undergraduate degree. In science, the first year is often spent providing you with the necessary facts that you'll need before you can move on to higher levels of analysis and synthesis of your own ideas. Much of this basic knowledge is therefore long-standing and well-understood. The nature of book publishing is such that the time between a book's beginnings in the mind of an author and the date it reaches a bookshop or library shelf can be several years, and so books are not a good way to publish up-to-date knowledge in fields of active research. Their use is in helping you with the basics: the laws and the dogma of your subject. Don't be afraid, then, to begin your research phase in a book.

No modern scientific textbook was ever designed to be read cover-to-cover. They are broken into chapters and subsections. This means you can go directly to a specific section after deciding what you want – or need – to find out. With the use of an index, you can narrow down your task to a single page without ever troubling yourself with the rest. A really well-produced book will have cues on the pages to help you skim-read: regular headings; subject-specific jargon in bold; regular cross-references to other explanations elsewhere in the book; and so on.

Bear in mind, also, that not everything in a textbook is meant to be understood by someone at your level. The first-year biology textbook at our own institution, for example, has concepts that aren't taught until final year, and even then only in one of the twenty or so different biology degrees. Don't be put off if you find concepts that are greatly removed from the level of detail taught by your course staff; the book authors didn't write the textbook specifically for someone on your degree, at your university, and in your year but, as long as you keep using your textbooks, you'll become better at spotting content at the appropriate level for you as time goes by.

Extracting just what you need

The really accessible textbooks authored with a university audience in mind will have several cues to help you decide where to dip in and out. This will help you be more efficient with your time when doing research for your written assignments.

The overall structure of a textbook is likely to be split into several broad parts. These will represent the overarching themes. Within these main parts you will normally find the chapters of the book. If you think of the themes as the equivalent of modules on your course, chapters might be the equivalent of individual lectures or small lecture series on particular topics. You might be told to read a chapter over the course of several days, perhaps to serve as an accompaniment to the material you're taught in class over a week. Chapters are the main divisions within a book, but it's useful to think about the internal structure of a chapter before you go reading through a whole as research for your essay.

Well-written subject textbooks may have summaries at the end of their chapters. These serve as the book's equivalent of the intended learning outcomes for your degree course. If you're looking for information on a specific topic, finding the relevant chapter and beginning to read is one way to proceed, but you might save yourself some time and effort by starting with the *last* page of the chapter to see what's in the summary. If the list of topics sounds very familiar to you at the start, take that as a cue that maybe you won't get as much return on your time-investment by choosing to read this section in lots of detail. Instead, perhaps you could be more efficient with your time by skipping straight to the pages within a chapter which are listed as covering concepts that are new to you, thus helping you to carry out your information gathering in a more focused way.

Look also at the way the information is presented. Is the book printed in such a way as to highlight the technical vocabulary you're supposed to be learning? If the pages feature text boxes with examples or definitions, or if the new subject-specific jargon is highlighted in bold font, and so on, think of these as the highlights and headlines of the chapter. You might be able to skim through the pages by only paying attention to these, again with the intention of identifying which pages are full of information you already know and which will teach you new concepts. When you find these, slow down and make a note of the information if it seems like it will be useful for your writing assignment.

Access

Your first port of call should be the physical shelves of your university library. If a text is listed by your university as 'recommended reading', they will almost certainly have it in their inventory. Books required for large courses will often be held as multiple copies, possibly in a short-loan section to ensure no student should have to wait too long to get access to it. Publishers of eBooks may make their texts available through your library, should your university pay for access on their students' behalf, and they may allow different levels of access. Some will only be viewable in a web browser. Some may be downloadable as PDFs with time limits on how many days the file will open before it refuses access and you need to go back to download it again, effectively limiting access to currently enrolled students. Some publishers may just make the eBooks available as standard PDFs, accessible forever after you download them, so take advantage of any of these you might come across while you still have your student login.

Journal articles

Uses

Journal articles are relatively short pieces of scientific communication from a group of researchers to the world at large. Publication of articles is the way scientists in academia build their careers. Someone might be making the most amazing breakthroughs, but if they never tell anyone about them, they won't be able to move forward for long. Without publishing, they won't be able to prove to anyone what they've done. Without proving what they've done, they won't be able to ask funding bodies for more money. Without money, they won't be able to pay for lab workers and equipment to continue the line of research. (A university doesn't actually pay its researchers: the researchers apply for grants of money to *pay the university* to keep the lights and the heating on, and, of course, to cover their own salaries.)

This is all important because it tells you something about what's going to be found in journal articles. They're going to contain discoveries that need to be shared with the scientific community so that everyone can move science forward, and things to impress funding bodies. What they're *not* going to contain are concisely presented lists of facts that will be useful for any one particular assignment.

This means you need to get into a habit of deciding what information you want from a journal article, looking for it in a targeted way, noting it, and then deciding where to go next.

Extracting just what you need

The standard format of a journal article is the same as for a lab report: Introduction, Materials and Methods, Results, and Discussion (IMRaD). (Sometimes the Discussion might be called a Conclusion, and sometimes both of these sections will be present. Structural nuances like this are usually not within the control of the authors, but are set out by the style guide of the journal to make sure all the articles that they accept and publish are equivalent.) Knowing where to find different types of information helps you to be more targeted with your information gathering for your assignment. Here's a list of common questions you might try to answer when reading a paper, and which part of it you'd focus on to get clarification:

Question/uncertainty/query/reason for reading	Section to read
Unsure whether an article is specific enough to the topic of your assignment?	**Introduction** – to check the background to the work and the aims.
You need to design your own experiments for an independent project.	**Materials and methods** – to see how a technique is carried out. Perhaps also **Results** to see the typical type of output.
You need to review literature, perhaps for a dissertation. In other words, you need to be able to briefly report other people's findings and summarise our current understanding of the field.	**Results** (see also subsection Evaluating and Refining Your Materials on p. 62 for more on judging the quality of someone else's findings, and Chapter 10 on critical analysis.)
	Conclusion/discussion – though these generally need to be read in conjunction with the **Results** section as Conclusions can contain generalities and theorising.

Table 7.1   Extracting just what you need from journal articles on a preliminary reading

These are places you might start reading in order to decide whether an article is worth reading in depth. Professional scientists rarely read an article from the first word to the last word in sequence, so we hope that by getting you into these same habits of looking quickly at the most relevant section for your purposes, you can more quickly decide whether to abandon reading an article that won't actually be of much value to you. Just remember that reporting on a scientist's conclusions without checking whether you believe that they are actually supported by their experimental data is a big scientific error. Assessing credibility is discussed further in Chapter 10 – Being Critical.

After you have found what you think to be the most crucial piece of information for your current requirements, you will need to go back and read the rest of the paper. This is where it becomes important to keep track of everything you've found so that you can formulate your own mental overview, and then integrate all of this with your writing. Holding on to lots of pieces of information on a variety of articles in your head quickly becomes an unmanageable task. We propose that, at the very least, you make a note of five bits of information on each paper in some kind of note. Different students we've worked with do this in different ways. It may be as simple as a piece of paper physically attached to the front of a printed article; it may be a spreadsheet that serves as the basis of a plan for your eventual essay; or it may be a project management app or website (you can read more about these on p. 62). The five minimum pieces of information we'd recommend that you note down are:

1 **Who wrote it, when, and where?** This is essentially the referencing information. You'll need to make sure you can pair up the notes with the article they refer to, should they become separated.
2 **What did the authors want to find?** What was the background to the article, and how would this new piece of research fill a gap in our previous knowledge?
3 **How did they do the investigation?** What methodology did they use?
4 **What did they find?** What was the major discovery? What were the individual discoveries that contributed to this?
5 **Do you believe them?** Does the data support the conclusions made at the end of the article? Can you find any reasons to doubt the validity of any parts of the authors' claims?

Again, these points will be expanded upon in Chapter 10 – Being Critical, but we reiterate them here because it's important for you to get into the habit of collecting these bits of information as you go along to make your job easier later. Don't feel you need to write these notes in a formal academic tone, or even in English, if that's not your native language. They should be helpful for you later and nobody else will ever need to read them, so if typing them in French, in Comic Sans font, on a pink background is what you prefer, then go for it.

While you're doing this, you might also find it useful to make a note of whether you found an article easy to read, or difficult, or boring. Think – even briefly – about why this is the case. Reflecting on your reading like this might help you think about good and bad academic style, and thus what you want to emulate or avoid in your own writing. Unexplained jargon and poorly labelled graphs are two classic examples we commonly hear about from our students. Use your reading, then, to inform the style you want to adopt yourself.

Access

A common way of discovering new articles is simply to start with the ones given as references by your lecturers, perhaps at the end of a class, or listed as recommended reading. Expand your knowledge base by following the references within those and broaden outwards into related articles. That way, you can be sure you're following a kind of historical chain showing how we've arrived at our current level of understanding instead of blindly searching online, which can be daunting if you've never done it before.

When you're ready to start doing your own database searches, don't just go to your favourite search engine and throw keywords into it. We cannot stress enough how important it is to think carefully about *where* you go to do your search, as well as *how* you carry it out.

Searching via library websites

Your library website almost certainly doubles as a searchable database of everything the library holds. Depending on the scale of your institution and the resource they've been able to invest in designing the webpages, you may be able to search not just for books, but for journals your university subscribes to, or it may go deeper and let you search for individual articles within those journals. Poke around on your website to see what functionality you have, and ask the librarians if you want them to explain anything for you.

Rather than someone who checks books in and out, the term 'librarian' at a university usually refers to someone with an in-depth knowledge of all of the resources available to students. They will negotiate deals with book publishers, buy books when new courses are offered by an institution, and will communicate with the people who run journals. You probably have different librarians who specialise in different subject areas. They're there to make your access to information easier, so don't be afraid to ask them or their assistants how your university's particular system works.

The benefit of accessing a journal via your library web pages is related to subscription fees and logins. Most peer-reviewed journals are not open-access (that is, they are not freely available to anyone) and so you either have to pay a membership fee, or pay-as-you-go to download the content. In paying your student fees, you are paying for the university to subscribe to all the major publishers on your behalf. Your subject librarians will be continually checking that all the relevant publishers for the degrees offered by your university are included in this list, and so by searching from your university web pages you are usually guaranteed to only get results from journals you have access to. This takes away the pain of searching by other means and finding yourself at a page asking you to pay $30.

In some cases, you may desperately need an article from a journal outside of your library's subscription list. It's worth approaching your subject librarian with details of the article and a justification for why you need it, and asking if they have a budget for such eventualities.

Searching via academic databases

Your university library's search pages are good for all of the reasons above, but they are usually necessarily generic, and may not have some of the more advanced and very useful functionality found in subject-specific academic databases.

Academic databases are essentially very specific search engines that return only results from reputable sources of academic literature, such as the publishers of peer-reviewed journal articles. Some examples of such databases include Web of Science, Chemical Abstracts, Scopus, and PubMed. These academic databases are the method of access that we hope you'd use because you can usually:

- be much more specific with your search terms and the search operators you put between them;
- tell the web page what *type* of information each search term is about (author, title, general keyword);
- specify the date range you're interested in;
- limit results to the type of article you want (primary research, review article, editorial, etc.).

… and they often allow you to do quite complex searches.

For example, you may try five or six different combinations of search terms before you decide which keywords are most effective, and then you may quickly compare the titles of primary research articles with those of reviews to get a feel for what's available. After experimenting like this for a while, you may decide the best results would come from combining the second and the fourth search strings you tried, as well as the date range you used on your fifth attempt, and the article type you specified in sixth search.

A good academic database will provide a history of your search strategy and allow you to combine your favourite elements to run one final 'super search'. Your library search page is unlikely to offer such a powerful tool. If any of your written assignments ever need to include a formal literature-review section, where you report on your findings from scientific publications before embarking upon your own discoveries, your work may benefit from a clear explanation of your search strategy. Using a good academic database with a thorough list of search functions like this will allow you to create this section demonstrating your rigour. Speak with your course staff to find out if and when this will be beneficial for your particular assignments.

Again, your university library will probably pay a subscription that allows you to use the most relevant academic databases in your subject, or perhaps to use extra features that would not be available to the general public. Different databases specialise in different areas (biology, chemistry, physics, etc.) so speak to your lecturers or your subject librarians about which database they'd recommend for your degree.

Search engines have trained us to trust the first results they show us. That's possible and reasonable because their algorithms will prioritise results on various criteria (such as which result people most often choose when they use the same search text you used, webpages and searches you've used recently, and an unknown number of other proprietary secret calculations that none of us are privy to). Academic databases, however, usually present you with the most recent results first. You need to be aware that the chances of these being the most relevant results for your particular purpose are extremely small.

General search engines have also trained us not to blink an eye when we see a number of results in the tens of thousands. With no default sorting in an academic database other than chronological order, finding what you actually need is like finding a needle in the proverbial haystack. Often, students just take what looks sort-of-reasonable from the first few pages of results, and make do with these.

Instead, you should think carefully about your search string. Can you add more terms to narrow it down? Can you use alternative words to mean the same thing? Can you use truncation with wild-card characters (these will be specific to each database, but commonly an asterisk is used) to catch alternative spellings or forms of a word (e.g. 'inflam*' instead to catch 'inflammation' and 'inflamed' as well as 'inflammatory')? Can you narrow down the years you're interested in? Do you need all types of paper, or are you perhaps just interested in review articles at this stage?

Find a search strategy that finds you several tens or hundreds of results only. Take a hot drink and half an hour to scan through the titles returned by this search, open the abstracts of the ones that sound interesting, and decide whether to download them for reading later. This will be far more effective for your knowledge and your grades in the long run than picking only those which were published most recently.

Keeping track of all your sources

Reference managers such as EndNote, Zotero, Mendeley, or ReadCube will help you keep a catalogue of all the journal articles you read in your student career. You can usually add notes to your catalogue entries, and most include a way to easily slot your references automatically into your documents as you type, which will save hours of your life.

Project management tools such as Evernote will help you keep different tasks organised with separate folders. You can collect all of the website URLs, lab data, images, and so on, into a folder alongside your essay draft, and access these from anywhere with an internet connection.

Evaluating and refining your materials

Not only is it difficult to know where to start, it's also difficult to know when to stop. In our day jobs, we are both regularly faced with students who have amassed large amounts of information but have not yet figured out how to create a sensible story, or extract the main findings from it all. It's important that you find a way to keep track of what you've discovered so that you can periodically step back and take an overview.

The good news for you is that not everything in that collection of thousands of websites and texts about your topic is worth your time reading, but the bad news is that not everything is as simple and objectively true as the scientists who discovered it would want. In this next section, we'll show you how to evaluate the usefulness of a source from the internet, from books, and from scientific journals. When you've finished this Chapter, we'd recommend that you also look at Chapter 10 – Being Critical for more detail on how to evaluate specific results and datasets.

After you've read this chapter, you will want to think about assembling your research into the skeleton for your own work. Structure will be covered in Part Three of this book.

Deciding what's useful

As we mentioned in the section on the uses of journal articles (p. 56), every scientist who writes an article has several masters to serve, and it's useful to be aware of these motivations so you can begin to recognise why you're being told certain things in articles. First, there is the simple desire to share what they've discovered with the wider scientific community. Second, there's the desire to show value for money to the body who funded the research grant that paid all of the lab costs. Third, there's the desire to progress the scientist's own career by having their article accepted into a journal with as high a reputation as possible.

Fourth, and increasingly as time passes, is the need to demonstrate all of these things to the academic host institution employing the scientist, as university staffing decisions rely more and more on the quality of publication records. Notice one thing: none of these reasons are related to producing education or training resources, both of which you are seeking in order to improve your writing.

Website authors, too, will have their own motivations for making information available to you. You might be looking for government policy documentation in order to compare it to the recommendations in the scientific research behind it, or for generic background information to help you decide what to search the academic databases for, or simply just to find teaching materials to help you revise your course content. All of these are legitimate reasons to search the general pool of information available online, and you need to be cautious about who wrote these pages and why.

Finally, when it comes to writing your own lab reports, you've got to cut through the potentially very large sets of results. Not all of this will be interesting to a reader, because they won't all answer the question you told them you were going to investigate in your introduction.

So what does all of this mean for you?

This means you will have to read with a critical eye and to look out for the specific parts of articles that seem relevant *to your topic*. Ask yourself why you chose to download or print an article. Are you interested in the methods the researchers used? In the question they tried to answer? In the findings you have read about in the abstract? If you can identify one of these things, you're in a much better position to read the paper without having to pore over every word and every detail. Note that this reading strategy is useful for saving time and deciding when to abandon an article during the *early* stages of your research. You must still assess all of the elements of an article On p. 58 we spoke about making short summary notes on what an article contained. We said you might want to note down:

1 The referencing information, in case your notes get separated from the article.
2 What the authors wanted to find out.
3 How they set about doing it.
4 What they reported.
5 Whether or not you believe them.

Let's look at this final point. It doesn't only relate to articles – you should assess the reliability of any information source you choose to use. This means looking at who wrote something (credibility), why they wrote it (purpose), and how long ago they wrote it (recency). We'll take those one at a time.

Evaluating credibility

Websites can clearly be written by anyone with a few dollars and some time. As with Wikipedia, there are no guarantees that a website author has any credentials in the subject. Take visual cues from the website that indicate how much time and effort has gone into its design, into securing a reasonable URL, and about how frequently it might be updated – that is, how professional the website's curation is. You may find 'About' sections with details of the person or organisation in charge of a website. Ask yourself whether anything in these details suggest that the authors are qualified to talk about the topic. Do they have academic credentials? Do they have experience working in a field? Generally speaking, experience alone is not regarded as giving much credibility, because all that guarantees is that an author has many anecdotes to draw on.

Books can similarly be written by just about anyone. With the rise of vanity publishing and automated self-publishing, anyone with enough money can publish a book on any topic they like. Finding something in print is not, therefore, a sign that it is any more reliable than something found online.

Take care to check the publisher's details before relying on a book for academic information. The books in your university library will all have been vetted by members of staff at the time of purchase, so you can put your faith in these. Academic publishers will send their books out for peer-review in the same way as journal editors do with articles. If you come across a book elsewhere, though, perhaps it'd be prudent to check you've heard of the publisher, or to look online to get a sense of how reputable they are and how many other books they have released in this field.

With both websites and books, be cautious of people who claim to have PhDs or Professorships in suspicious-sounding topics. Qualifications can be given by online organisations with little, if any, evidence of someone's ability. Dr Ben Goldacre, medical doctor and science-communication columnist for the Guardian newspaper, famously purchased a certified professional membership of the American Association of Nutritional Consultants in the name of his dead cat, Henrietta, for the price of $60 (Goldacre, 2007).

You can generally trust that someone who publishes in a scientific journal knows what they are talking about, as journals usually rely on a rigorous system of peer-review. This means that any time a scientist submits their experimental report to a journal for consideration, it is sent out by the journal's editor to other experts in that specialism. They get a chance to check that the methodology was appropriate for the question being asked, that the appropriate controls were used, that the conclusions are reasonable given the results observed, and generally get to critique any problems they can see. If they recommend that more lab work must be done or that sections need to be rewritten, it can be returned to the author(s), who get a chance to address those deficiencies and resubmit. At this stage, if the article passes the requirements of the peer-reviewers and the journal editor, it can be published.

There's little more you can add to this fairly robust system, except perhaps to check the background of the journal itself. Unfortunately, there has been a recent trend of bogus journals reaching out to scientists to ask for submissions, rather than waiting for scientists to approach with work that's ready to be seen. This lowers the bar for quality, and introduces to the market scientific articles that are not as reliable. Several investigative reports have established that some of these new journals will submit anything they can get their hands on; even nonsense articles generated automatically by computer algorithms stitching together sufficiently academic-sounding sentences (van Noorden, 2014)!

But, overwhelmingly, if you find an article in a peer-reviewed journal, you can trust in its authorship. (Note that while the authors may be credible, this does not guarantee their research is perfect.)

Evaluating purpose

If you're arrived at an informative webpage from a search engine or any other link, spend a few minutes looking at the website's main pages and ask yourself why it exists. Does it have a shop? It's extremely common in the biological sciences, for example, to find websites selling supplements, and their sales are supported by extensive pages claiming to be scientific information about their effectiveness. If the author has any agenda other than the publication of science, you may have to assume that anything they've written is biased in favour of supporting that other goal.

Similarly, books can be self-published in order to further a career, or to indirectly generate interest in an author so that people research them, find their website, and end up buying something.

Then there are categories of grey-areas, such as charities and support groups for people suffering from conditions or lobbying for changes in laws. These websites may be full of genuinely appropriate and authoritative pieces of information, and it can be difficult for you to tell when this is the case. If in doubt, avoid these sources.

Peer-reviewed articles are, again, likely to be safe in this regard. Any conflicts of interest should be declared in a note somewhere near the start or the end of any article. The advice we gave in the section above on Evaluating Credibility also applies here.

Evaluating on the basis of recency

The age of an article, book, website, or other material does not in itself cast doubt upon its validity. By nature, though, science is a progressing and self-correcting field, and anything from more than perhaps a couple of years in the past has possibly been superseded by a new, better, more in-depth, more rigorous, or otherwise superior understanding. There isn't a cut-off point at which we'd regard a source to be out-of-date, as this entirely depends on the kind of information being presented. The structure of DNA, for example, is still a double-helix, just as it was when it was discovered in 1953. We know a lot more detail about this, though, and you would let yourself down if you found the 1953 article and ignored all of the research between then and now, and your grades would suffer accordingly.

Your tutors and lecturers will be able to give you an idea of a reasonable period from which to source your information on a given topic.

Categorising your reading list

As you go along (note: that's worth repeating – *as you go along*), make time to think about what larger messages you're getting from everything you've read. Try to decide whether you could mentally categorise an article under a heading that you'd find useful later when drafting. You might like to group your articles by the topics they discussed. You might want to classify them according to their age. You might think about comparing all the articles that use a certain methodology and contrasting those with articles that use a different one. Let's take an example of papers in the field of human diseases. Table 7.2 shows some ways you might like to classify them:

Themes	Examples of category names you could use
Topic	Normal biology/disease biology/good or bad treatment outcome
Recency	Last 3 years/3–10 years/more than 10 years old
Reliability	Large sample size, etc. (see Chapter 10 for more)
Type of publication	Review/systematic review/primary experiment (see Chapter 10 for more)
Methodology	Petri dish experiments/mouse model/patient drug treatment
Conclusion	Recommends/advises against the use of a new technique

Table 7.2 Categories to help manage your reading list

Hopefully, you can see that by placing your reading into groupings like these, a sort of natural division of ideas begins to emerge. You might start to count the number of papers in favour of a new treatment, the number against it, and then this could help you think about what your essay or dissertation's overarching message will be. You might even be able to go to the level of planning individual paragraph topics on the basis of the categories.

If you do this categorisation *as you go along,* you'll find that writing the work itself becomes far less difficult to start and far less daunting.

Selecting material generated from your own scientific research

In this section we'll discuss the distinction between experiments you would want to write up in a report, and those which are carried out as preliminary 'pilot' studies to test that a procedure works. As with any of your writing tasks, it's sensible to begin by asking you to think about what your marker wants to see.

In first or second-year undergraduate labs, the purpose is often to show you how a particular technique works. This will typically be done in a very controlled way, that is, based on an experiment with a predictable outcome so that you're in no doubt as to whether you've mastered the technique (examples of this include the production of crystals of a chemical product with a known melting point, or the measurement of the gravitational constant, or the cutting of DNA into fragments of an expected length). In write-ups of these simple types of labs, your marker probably wants to see evidence that you can write in the correct tone and format for your discipline, and that you can relate the outcomes of your experiment to the rules and theories that govern your subject. This means you should probably place emphasis on the style of your writing, the 'clean-ness' of your data formatting, and the connections between your data and the introduction – where you introduce a principle – and the conclusion – where you relate your findings back to it.

As you move through your degree, you'll usually be given more and more autonomy, both over exactly what you *do* in the lab and in how you select what goes into your write-up. Depending on your year of study, the write-up might be called a lab report, a project report, or a dissertation (some subjects see dissertations as lab-based rather than literature-based; if you're not sure of the distinction, see Chapter 4). The more autonomy you have had, the more decisions you will need to make about which experiments are worth reporting to your marker. Again, ask yourself what they are looking for.

If you have arrived at a definitive conclusion, this should be your main finding and you should focus on describing this.

If your main results were more open-ended because maybe you didn't definitively prove or disprove a hypothesis one way or another, or perhaps you got the answer you wanted but this then opened up another question to be asked, then the main thrust of your report would be a presentation of your results with a discussion around the future of the research.

If your experiments actually led you to conclude nothing, then your report would be based around showing everything you attempted. (We personally know a PhD student who spent three years trying to show how a gene worked. The gene was known to help crops tolerate high temperatures, and was therefore appealing to genetic engineers trying to feed the world. The student showed that the gene held the instructions for a specific protein, but was completely unable to show what the protein did, which other proteins it interacted with, any specific part of the cell that it was found in, or any other biotechnologically useful features. The student did everything they could have been expected to do, though, and now has a PhD – the highest degree a university can give – and is working as a postdoctoral researcher with a successful career.) As long as your report demonstrates that you're a proficient scientist-in-training with a sensible approach to solving the problems you faced, you can still attain top marks.

With that said, avoid including negative results unless you really have no other choice, or unless those negative results tell you something unexpected and then form the justification for a change of project direction. A marker is unlikely to be interested in any initial test experiments you carried out to check that a technique would work; they may, however, be interested in the optimisation steps you took if you were designing your own experimental procedure completely from scratch. Perhaps you used a piece of equipment to counterbalance something heavy in a 'homemade' setup, or you knew you had to carry out a new and unique process at a very specific temperature. Perhaps you could tell from first principles and logic that a range of values would work but you weren't sure what weight or what temperature would work *best*. If you tried a range of values and then used the best one for the rest of your actual tests, your marker is likely to be interested in seeing how you arrived at that decision. A graph of weight, or temperature, plotted against the effectiveness of your innovative procedure would make a valuable contribution to your report.

What underpins all of our advice on how to select material from your own experiments is the idea that your markers want to see that you are becoming a good trainee scientist. Conciseness is valued, so they don't want to see unnecessary detail about pilot experiments. Logical thinking is valued, so they will want to see how you solved problems with the larger theory behind your experiments. Finally, clarity is valued, so if you are including things like images, ask yourself whether a newcomer to your research will easily arrive at the same conclusion as you based on the quality of the figures you include. For more on data presentation, see Chapter 9 – Working with Data.

Incorporating and Referencing Other People's Work

Top 3 staff comments on incorporating other people's work:

▶ A lack of references tells us the student hasn't done further reading around the topic.

▶ It's obvious that the student hasn't learned this for themselves; they've used a thesaurus to help write a direct quotation in disguise.

▶ The best students use other people's work as a basis to support their own descriptions, arguments, or logic.

Top 3 student comments on incorporating other people's work:

▶ How do I actually mention other people's work in my sentences; do I just cite a source at the end of the paragraph?

▶ How many references do I need for an assignment of this length?

▶ Which referencing format should I use?

If you've read the previous two chapters, you'll be familiar with the mechanics of how to find materials to base your own writing upon. It's important for you to start thinking about how you would write about those sources in your essays, lab reports, and dissertations.

Why incorporate the work of others at all?

The answer to this depends very much on the type of piece you're writing. (For an explanation of the most common words used to define your task, which we'll call Command Words in these next few pages, see Table 3.2 on p.24.) Table 8.1 explains the rationale for giving you different types of assignment, and shows how referencing can help you to demonstrate your fulfilment of those aims.

How references support different types of assignment
Assignment type: Descriptive essay
Typical command words: Describe, Outline, List, Explain, Detail
Purpose of assignment: • To test that you know the basic facts of your field
Commonly used: • Early years of your degree in particular, but may also still feature as an element of exam hall essays through to final year
Reasons for you to use references: • To show you have engaged in independent study and carried out further reading • To provide evidence that what you've said is correct
Assignment type: Evaluative essay
Typical command words: Evaluate, Compare and Contrast, Justify, Assess the Use of
Purpose of assignment: • To show you can distinguish good science from bad, or a good methodology from a better one, or a more realistic conclusion from a more farfetched one • To show you can compare, evaluate, and come up with your own ideas and opinions about a topic *based on evidence*
Commonly used: • Later stages of your undergraduate degree / immediately on a master's degree
Reasons for you to use references: • To show where the boundaries sit between facts you've read about and opinions you've come to regarding their validity • To give credit to the scientists who carried out the experiments • To help the reader follow which findings are from which scientist – especially important if your piece of writing is comparing two or more sources and you frequently change from one to the other
Assignment type: Lab report
Typical command words: N/A – lab titles may or may not have command words
Purpose of assignment: To test whether you can: • Design and carry out tests based on evidence about what methodologies have worked in the past and might work now • Link theory with findings • Put your findings in the context of the wider scientific community's current state of knowledge

Table 8.1 Types of assignment, and how use of referencing relates to their purpose

Commonly used: • Throughout all stages of a degree, but referencing becomes particularly necessary in higher years when you have an element of control over the design of your experiments, and you may start to build directly upon the work of others
Reasons for referencing: • To show your marker where you read about the background information you used to justify your experiments   • To allow a reader to follow up on that background if they wish   • To be open and transparent in your conclusion and discussion section when you're describing whether your results agree or disagree with what others have found   • To begin to join the academic community of science discussion, rather than to keep writing up your own findings in isolation from all others
Assignment type: Self-directed dissertation
Typical command words: N/A – the research question should come from you
Purpose of assignment: • To test whether you can develop your own investigative questions and ideas, and carry out independent library research
Commonly used: • In the later stages of a degree
Reasons for referencing: • Same as for evaluative and descriptive essays, but there will likely be many more references in a piece of work of this size and complexity

Table 8.1 *(Continued)*

All of these reasons for incorporating the work of others are unified by these general principles: authority, correctness, openness, clarity, and giving credit. Many of our own students are concerned about being accused of plagiarism and think of referencing as a technical operation that helps you avoid being accused of it. Our aim is to help you feel less like this is a matter of rules and punishment, and more like it's a convention or a writing style that marks you as an academic. Professional researchers don't tend to think about plagiarism when they write their papers; they think more in terms of pre-empting any readers who might think to themselves, 'how do we know that?' or 'prove it!'. In the same way, we hope you'll come to think of referencing as a way of marking yourself as a student who has read widely and can back up their assertions with proof.

For this reason, it's crucial that you think carefully about how you select your sources. They must be authoritative, reliable, and appropriate to your discipline.

That means choosing a good scientific database with which to carry out your searches (not just Google Scholar), avoiding sources whose primary purpose for existing is to promote something (for example, a small campaigning body, some charities, and anyone selling a product), and ensuring that the sources you choose to reference also mention *their own* sources of information. For more detail on how to decide whether a source is reliable, see Chapter 7 – Researching the Topic and Evaluating Your Materials , and Chapter 10 – Being Critical.

Commonly used referencing terms and their meanings

The language we use to describe referencing uses a few words that are not commonly used in everyday English, so it's worth defining them here first.

Citation: Any note in the body of a text that directs the reader's attention to the fact that there is an external source of information. Common examples are the name-and-date format:

> The sky is blue (Boyle and Ramsay, 2016)

... or the numbered format:

> The sky is blue.[1]

Reference: The full set of details about an external source, sufficient to let a reader track down a copy of that source for themselves. Usually located at the end of an article/book/chapter.

Endnote: A supplementary piece of information supplied at the end of an article/book/chapter. Not common in the sciences. Usually only seen as reference lists at the end of each chapter in large textbooks. (Not to be confused with EndNote, the bibliography management tool – see subsection Keeping Track of All Your Sources on p.62 for more.)

Footnote: A supplementary piece of information supplied at the bottom of a page. Marginally more common than endnotes, but still not common in the physical and biological sciences. You may find these in some articles if your field crosses over into governmental policy and legal documents.

Article: A single complete piece of writing, usually reporting the findings of a piece of research. This type is referred to as primary research. Other examples of article types are reviews (which summarise many other articles) and editorials (where a journal editor discusses a contemporary topic of active research). A collection of **articles** is published in each **issue** of a **journal**.

Journal: A publication that takes submissions from scientists, submits them (usually) to a process of peer-review, and publishes those submissions that pass the review process as articles. Editions are usually published at regular intervals (e.g. weekly, monthly, quarterly, biannually, annually, and so on; see also **volumes** and **issues**).

Issue: An individual copy of a **journal**, containing several **articles**. Usually published at regular intervals. Sequentially numbered. If a **journal** is issued more than once per year, a **volume** number will also be used.

Volume: A collection of journal **issues** from one whole year. If a particular journal only publishes one issue per year, the concept of a volume does not apply.

Impact factor: A measure of the quality or importance of a journal (note: not an article). Calculated each year by looking back at all the articles published by that journal in the two previous years, adding up the number of times every article from those two years had been cited by someone else so far in the current year, then dividing this total number of citations by the number of articles. An impact factor of 2 means that, on average, each article from the previous two years has been cited twice. Higher impact factors can be taken to mean that a journal has a reputation for selecting and publishing more groundbreaking research articles, as they are used as the basis for other people's works more frequently than articles from journals with lower impact factors.

Quoting: Writing someone else's words, marking them in quotation marks, and citing the source. Not often used in science. (See p.74 – Quoting, below.)

Paraphrasing: Taking someone else's ideas, changing the wording, and citing the original source. Not good practice. (See p.75 – Paraphrasing a Source, below.)

Summarising: Taking the pieces of someone else's work that are the most relevant to your own piece of writing, explaining the ideas in your own words to show you have understood, and citing the original source. The only real method of properly using someone else's work in your own. (See p.76 – Summarising a Source, below.)

Incorporating other people's work into your writing

As we mentioned above, there is a spectrum of different ways you can write about someone else's work in your piece. The spectrum ranges from direct copying without any attribution, which is (hopefully) obviously wrong, through to using a collection of sources that complement each other in order to justify your view on a topic and your original thought. In these next pages we'll start by explaining what a citation is and what it looks like. Then we'll show you how to build your sentence structure around a citation in various ways along this spectrum of correctness. Lastly, we'll show you what's required of a full reference list at the end of your written work.

Quoting

> The successful landing of humans on the moon and emergence from the landing vehicle onto the lunar surface represented one small step for [a] man; one giant leap for mankind.

With no attributions, we have to assume this writer intended for this sentence to be interpreted in the same way as any other in their essay, that is, as one of their own. Hopefully you will recognise this famous line from Neil Armstrong, the first person on the moon, and will agree that this represents a case of obvious plagiarism. It could, however, be argued that this is such a famous line that no-one would think the writer intended to pass it off as their own work. Here is a more subtle example; this time, a hypothetical report from the World Health Organization:

> **Original source:** The issue of how governments respond to the challenges posed by climate change becomes more urgent with each passing year. Maximum temperatures in subtropical farmland areas are expected to rise. Rainfall patterns are expected to be disturbed. Atmospheric CO_2 levels continue to increase, altering the rate at which crops can extract carbon in order to grow. All of these factors must be modelled in combination if we are to create realistic projections relating to food security over the coming decades.
> **Student's work (plagiarism):** Climate change is obviously an important issue for food production because maximum temperatures in subtropical farmland areas are expected to rise, rainfall patterns are expected to be disturbed, and atmospheric CO_2 levels continue to increase, altering the rate at which crops can extract carbon in order to grow.

This is extremely bad practice, as the student could be given university credit for high-level thinking that they had not actually done. If plagiarism like this is detected later – even years later – it can have serious consequences for the qualification the author holds.

The quote would be improved by the use of quotation marks and a proper citation, such as this (we will use Harvard style):

> **Student's work (quotation):** Climate change is obviously an important issue for people and industries involved in food production. 'Maximum temperatures in subtropical farmland areas are expected to rise. Rainfall patterns are expected to be disturbed. Atmospheric CO_2 levels continue to increase, altering the rate at which crops can extract carbon in order to grow' (World Health Organization, 2016). All of these factors could have an impact on the food output of farms.

While this is no longer an example of plagiarism, it's still just extremely lazy work. If you check the wording of your university's assessment rules, you may find a part that explains what students must demonstrate in order to be granted a passing grade. It's unlikely that an essay built on a foundation of quotations will get a high grade (or perhaps even pass at all). This is because it's possible to write a paragraph by copying words in this way yet without ever demonstrating that you understand what those statements mean, or how they relate to each other. It's for this reason that quoting – at least in the sciences – is highly discouraged.

It would be slightly better for you to put things into your own words. Moving along the spectrum from the most extreme kinds of unacceptable practices in the direction of slightly better ones, we come to paraphrasing.

Paraphrasing a source

If you have read something and understood what it means, you'll be able to explain it to someone without looking back at the original source. Many students get into the bad habit of practising this using a thesaurus. They work under the impression that changing the wording so it is different from that used by the original author will be enough to avoid plagiarism. It is not. Neither is dissecting a sentence into its separate parts (clauses) and reorganising them into a new sentence structure. By doing this, a writer is simply taking statements and finding ways to try to cheat their way through the academic system. They are looking for legitimate ways to say someone else's ideas without giving them their credit. An example might look like this:

Original source: The issue of how governments respond to the challenges posed by climate change becomes more urgent with each passing year. Maximum temperatures in subtropical farmland areas are expected to rise. Rainfall patterns are expected to be disturbed. Atmospheric CO_2 levels continue to increase, altering the rate at which crops can extract carbon in order to grow. All of these factors must be modelled in combination if we are to create realistic projections relating to food security over the coming decades.

Student's work (paraphrased): Climate change is obviously an important issue for people and industries involved in food production. The highest temperatures experienced each year in subtropical farmland areas are expected to go up. Patterns of rain are expected to change. Crops extract carbon from the air in order to grow, and an increasing level of carbon dioxide could have an effect on the rate at which they do this (World Health Organization, 2016). All of these factors could have an impact on the food output of farms.

Again, this is lazy work. If you check your university's marking rules, you will see that this does not fulfil the requirements placed upon you to demonstrate university-level understanding of a topic.

Summarising a source

Instead of quoting or paraphrasing, what you should aim to do is to be able to explain the concept in a way that is entirely from your own mind. That might mean extracting only a few pieces of the original text, focusing on only those which are useful for your particular assignment – in other words, summarising. For example, if your essay is about how a hinge joint like the elbow is different from a ball-and-socket joint like the hip and you've found a useful information source, you needn't explain all of the details from that source about all of the different tissue types found in bone. The author might have explained these tissue types, but that goes beyond the scope of your answer about joint shape and movement. Remember that the author of the source you're using had their own reasons for writing their article or book chapter, and your task is to answer an essay question or write a report on something that this author had no involvement in. You therefore probably don't need to include everything they said.

As well as writing a shorter summary, another practical way to make the words your own is to separate the act of making notes and the act of writing your own piece of work into different days. This allows you some time to forget the full, exact *wording* and makes it easier to write from a memory of the *concepts* instead. Perhaps, if you're only going to use the notes as an aide for drafting your work, you'd find it useful to only write them in bullet-point form, or create a diagram or flow-chart. This will help you encapsulate the ideas without using the full, original phrasing. Here's an example of such a diagram:

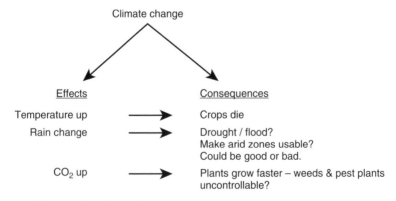

Figure 8.1   Example notes made from a source

Note how none of this is made of sentences, but it contains enough detail to cover the main concepts and so it would be very easy to construct a new version later. It also contains some original thoughts. Here's how a final, non-plagiarised, summary version might look:

Original source: The issue of how governments respond to the challenges posed by climate change becomes more urgent with each passing year. Maximum temperatures in subtropical farmland areas are expected to rise. Rainfall patterns are expected to be disturbed. Atmospheric CO_2 levels continue to increase, altering the rate at which crops can extract carbon in order to grow. All of these factors must be modelled in combination if we are to create realistic projections relating to food security over the coming decades.

Student's work (summarised): Climate change is obviously an important issue for people and industries involved in food production. Changing temperatures, rainfall, and atmospheric CO_2 levels could all have an effect on farm output (World Health Organization, 2016). It is unclear whether these effects would lead to positive or negative consequences as some would be beneficial and some detrimental to a farmer, but it's clear that all of these factors could contribute in some way to a change in the rate of food production. It is important that we concentrate on all of these factors together, rather than individually, if we are to plan effectively to deal with the change.

Not only has the paragraph from the World Health Organization report been summarised down to a single sentence, but the student has gone beyond simply reporting what they've found and has used this research to make their own interpretations and predictions.

Phrases to use when incorporating someone else's work

It can become tedious to introduce someone else's research if you always use the same phrases to do it. (It can also become tedious for your markers to read...) Scientific language should be simple and unambiguous, but that does not mean it should be so repetitive as to risk losing your reader's attention. Here's a list of phrases you might like to use to vary your sentence construction while still writing in an appropriately academic tone:

• According to Ramsay (2016), the sky is blue.
• The sky is blue (Ramsay, 2016).
• As was shown in a recent study, the sky is blue (Ramsay, 2016).
• This contrasts with other results which suggest that the sky is blue (Ramsay, 2016).
• This is in accordance with other results which suggest that the sky is blue (Ramsay, 2016).
• Several recent studies have suggested that the sky is blue (Boyle, 2015; Ramsay, 2016).
• Several recent conflicting studies have shown that the sky may be blue (Ramsay, 2016), red (Boyle, 2015), or black (Smith, 2016), depending on the time of day when the observation is made.
• While an author of one study was uncertain as to the consistency of their research, they did conclude that the sky is usually observed to be blue (Ramsay, 2016).

These examples should show you that it's possible to mention the author, or authors, of a text in the flow of your sentences to help you make a point about how their findings fit in with the wider scientific conversation. If you are using a numbered format for your citations rather than the author-date format demonstrated here, you can still use the name of an author in the flow of your text as long as you include the usual number in the appropriate place too. The final example in particular might seem unusual as it talks explicitly about 'an author' – and we are traditionally taught to avoid mentioning people – but the important feature here is that the uncertainty about the results was *that author's own* conclusion. In such a case, it is necessary to mention them personally in order to give them credit. Compare that final example with this other attempt to say exactly the same thing:

One author concluded that the sky is usually observed to be blue (Ramsay, 2016), though there is uncertainty as to the consistency of their research.

This makes it appear that the critique was not Ramsay's, but was a new thought on the part of the student. Make an effort at your proofreading stage to avoid ambiguities and examples of accidental plagiarism such as this.

Major referencing styles in science

You'll have noticed that all of our example citations have mentioned an author's surname and a year. Different subjects have come to use different styles of references. This is important for you to know if you're studying subjects in different disciplines, as you'll need to use the correct style convention for each class. It's also useful to know so you can be prepared if you ever need to read outside of your core field.

Even within the sciences you will find variations on the main styles. We won't explain the precise details of how these different referencing systems work because some of the styles are dictated by professional bodies and the guidelines are regularly updated. Some styles simply have many subtle variations which are colloquially referred to under the same name. Instead, here in Table 8.2 we'll explain the pros and cons of the two main categories of scientific referencing styles so that you'll understand why they're used, and perhaps that will give you a better idea of how, when, and why to use them in your own writing.

Broad categories of reference styles used in science
Category: Name-date
Examples of in-text citation: • The sky is blue (Ramsay, 2016). • According to Ramsay (2016), the sky is blue.
Strengths: • Author name immediately visible • Date immediately visible • Able to incorporate name into flow of sentence, giving flexibility
Weaknesses: • Interrupts the visual flow of a sentence on a page
Examples of name-date styles: • Harvard • Chicago • APA (American Psychological Association)
Category: Numbered
Example of in-text citation: • The sky is blue.[1] • The grass is green.[1]

Table 8.2   Examples of the main citation and referencing styles

Strengths: • Easy to read through; doesn't interrupt flow
Weaknesses: • Can't assess author or recency without turning to references list at the end • difficult to remember which referenced source was about which topic, which is useful if a source is used several times at different points throughout a piece of writing – easier to associate this with a name. **Examples of numbered styles:** Vancouver

Table 8.2 *(Continued)*

In the sciences, we predominantly use one of these two categories rather than putting footnotes at the bottom of pages within the body of a text. This is probably because our journal articles are typically very short – usually fewer than ten pages – and so it is relatively easy to turn to the end and look at the full reference list. The footnote style is used more in disciplines where publications commonly take the form of books, and where accessing the back pages can be more cumbersome.

Citations – the parts within your text

The general advice in citing is to put the citation as close to your first mention of that work as possible. That helps you delineate where a report of what was contained in the article finishes, and where your comments on it begin.

The difficulty comes in placing a citation within a paragraph that is mainly made up of details of whatever you find in a source. Should a citation still come at the end? Should it come after you've said the name of the author within the flow

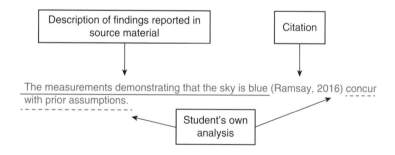

Figure 8.2 Components of an in-text citation

of your sentences? Should it come after the first sentence of the paragraph? There is no hard-and-fast rule about this, but there are some principles to bear in mind.

> In a recent study, the colour of the sky was measured to be blue (Ramsay, 2016). The colour profile changed slightly as the day progressed from mid-morning to early evening, but it largely remained in the same part of the spectrum. After 5pm, the colour shifted towards the red.

This paragraph contains technical information which could only have come from the article already cited after the first sentence, and there is nothing possessive in the language to suggest that the writer is making a claim to it themselves. It's also in the past tense, which indicates the author of the essay is reporting something concrete which already happened, rather than making a statement of their own current, ongoing knowledge. Therefore, the educated reader will infer that what comes after the citation is also from that same source report. If you wanted to improve this to remove all doubt, it might be preferable to begin the second sentence with a pronoun to refer to the authors: 'They observed that the colour profile ... '

Contrast that with a similar paragraph on the same topic where the citation comes at the very end:

> The sky was recently shown to be blue. During the course of the day, the colour remained largely the same, as was expected, based on preliminary observations conducted by eye. The colour shifted, however, in the evening, when a red tinge became more and more prominent. The spectrophotometers also detected a spike in UV light levels, which were not noticed by eye as this is outside of the visual range (Ramsay, 2016).

It's far less obvious what the citation refers to now. Is it the final nugget of information about UV being invisible to the naked eye? Is it the spike in UV light detected in the evening? Is it the shift from blue towards red? Is it the consistent blue colouration throughout the day? Is it all of the above? As we saw from the previous example paragraph, it refers to everything *except* the visibility of UV to the naked eye, but by placing the citation at the end of the whole paragraph, it is impossible to clear up this uncertainty.

Hopefully you can see why positioning is so important, and why your common sense is often a better guide than any hard-and-fast rule we might provide you with.

Now that you've seen the basic mechanics of how and where to incorporate a citation, we'll look at the subtleties of how to report on the contents of that source in your own words.

References – the list at the end

The citations in the body of your text are just signposts; simple marks embedded in your text to show your reader that some information has come from somewhere else. This is never enough to reliably let your reader find that exact source, and so you must complement it with the full referencing information at the end.

There are no hard-and-fast rules for you to follow in order to create your reference list, and the specifics are subject to change over time. For example, one of the most famous and widely used referencing styles, APA, is written and periodically updated by the professional body that shares its name (the American Psychological Association). At the time of writing (2016), if their rough pattern of issuing updated editions is to continue (1974, 1984, 1994, 2001, 2009), they would be expected to publish new guidelines within the next few years. You will also find that different universities can place their own extra requirements on top of a 'standard' referencing style. Instead of trying to teach you these subtle variations – which are crucial but are mostly to do with which parts should be italicised, which should be in bold, where the commas and full stops should go, and so on – we'll show you what the most common elements of a reference are, why they're useful to a reader, and how to tell them apart when you see them yourself. Your own institution will then be able to tell you which precise variation on a standard format they wish you to use.

Referencing textbooks

A reference for a textbook would look something like this:

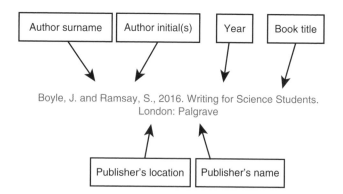

Figure 8.3   Components of a reference for a book

The authors, date, and title information allow a reader to do a quick search on a database at a library or bookshop. The name of the publishing house allows the reader to make contact with the people who hold the master copies and who may be able to give information on where to find books that are old, out of print, or otherwise rare and difficult to find. The location makes it easier to track down a publisher, and can also help distinguish between offices of large publishing houses in different countries, as not every book is printed for every market around the world. Different editions for different locations may have slightly different contents. If your reader were to follow your reference and pick up a copy from a different part of the world, they may not be able to find the exact material you cited. By including the publisher's location in your reference list you can help explain why this difference may arise, and this avoids any improper accusation that you might have made things up.

If your book is a large one on varied topics – and many introductory university textbooks are – check the first few pages to see if the chapters have each been contributed by separate specialist authors. You may know your textbook by the names of the author(s) listed on the front cover, when in fact they oversaw the editing process of combining many contributors' works. In such cases where you can identify the author or authors of an individual chapter, a reference should look something like this:

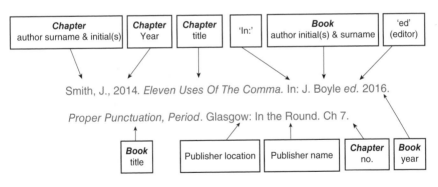

Figure 8.4 Components of a reference for a chapter in a book with editors

You will notice there are two years included here. The year of chapter authorship may be different from the year the book was published, as the chapter may have been carried over from a previous edition, or the book may have simply taken a long time to assemble.

Referencing journal articles

A reference for a journal article would look something like this:

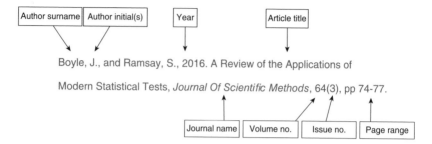

Figure 8.5 Components of a reference for a journal article

The standard convention is that a new volume number will be used each year. For journals that publish more than once per year, a second numbering system is used as well. Thus, within each volume you might find multiple issues. Providing your reader with a volume number is useful, but including an issue number makes your reference more precise.

Imagine you were given a stack of print editions of a journal which publishes an edition every three months. The stack contains every issue from the last five years. Imagine, also, that you know you have to find a very particular piece of information attributed to an author of one of the articles somewhere in that stack. How easy would it be to find the original sentences?

If you start off knowing the name of the author and the year they published their finding, you could take the issues from that year and scan through their tables of contents until you find what you're looking for. But what if the author publishes more than one article in the journal in that year? And what if two authors with the same surname publish in that same year?

If you're given the title of the article and the page range it occupies, you could either scan the tables of contents looking for the title, or you could directly turn to those page numbers in every issue in the stack. You'll eventually find the article, but that's still more time consuming than would be ideal.

If you're given the author's name, the article's title, and the volume number, then we're really getting somewhere. A volume number is not as specific as an issue number, though, so we still won't have been able to jump easily and immediately to the specific location of the article.

Of course, as your literature searching is almost certainly going to take place online, and you can do keyword searches instead of manually looking up editions, these issues may seem trivial. The difficulty comes when a search page doesn't quite behave the way you expect it to (because it's not Google, and perhaps it has its own unique search algorithm you've never faced before), or when you appear to have found a result but you find yourself blocked from following the link. (This can happen when your university library login details aren't recognised by the publisher's website, perhaps because you're not on campus and you're therefore connecting from an unexpected IP address, or perhaps the login you used on the database hasn't been seamlessly communicated to the journal's website, or perhaps for one of any number of other unanticipated technological reasons.)

At times like these, you need to know how to interpret a full reference in order to be able to access the article quickly, reliably, and without the help of an academic literature database or search engine. For more on how to search for literature, see Chapter 7. It's important, too, that you learn how to adopt these referencing conventions in your own scientific writing.

Referencing journal articles accessed online

We haven't distinguished how to reference print vs online versions of articles as there is simply no need to. In the interest of clarity, precision, and historical consistency, full referencing details for the *print* version of an article are always required, no matter the access method. You may be familiar with conventions for referencing online materials such as including the URL and the date you accessed a web page. These extra details are optional but unnecessary when it comes to journal articles.

URLs for journal articles

Referencing just the title of the article with the URL and access date probably wouldn't even work for anyone except you. Since journals are usually behind paywalls (which your library pays for on your behalf) the URL that you reach may contain elements that identify you as a paid user. These elements will not work for anyone else (or perhaps even for you, if you log out).

Dates of access for journal articles

Journal articles are fixed pieces of scientific writing, so a date of access has really no relevance. The authors will not be able to return to the article and make changes. This is by design, and ensures openness for all readers in the future. Corrections and additions can be published later if the author considers it necessary in light of new information. These corrections would be published separately, though, rather than as changes to the original article. These new bulletins would also be given full referencing details of their own. If you wish to use an article as a source for your own writing, and a crucial element that you're using comes from a later correction, make sure you cite and reference both the original and the correction as separate publications.

Conclusion

Having read this chapter, we hope that you will:

- understand how to find and use appropriate materials;
- understand how to use others' work as supporting evidence, not replacements, for your own ideas;
- understand referencing in the wider context of sound, professional academic practice;
- be well-equipped to avoid plagiarism, due to a deeper understanding of how and why we use other people's work.

Working with Data

Top 3 staff comments on data:

▶ Figures and tables are often poorly laid out on the page, making them difficult or cumbersome to read.

▶ Data is presented but not referred to in the text, or it isn't labelled properly.

▶ Certain types of data are completely unsuitable for certain types of graph or table, so it's important to know what you're trying to show.

Top 3 student comments on data:

▶ I've been making graphs since high school. I know how to label my figures.

▶ How much do I need to repeat in the main text?

▶ I had no idea organising my data in my report would take so long!

Returning to the findings of our research we mentioned in Chapter 2 – The Lab Report, 50% of lecturers said the purpose of assigning you lab reports was to help improve your communication skills. In your degree, you'll make thousands of measurements. It's up to you to decide which of those are (a) relevant to the story you're trying to tell in any given assessment, and (b) useful and comprehensible from the point of view of your reader. In this chapter, we'll show you what we hope you will do and why, and we'll try to show you how to avoid the common pitfalls.

Why data presentation is important

Scientific writers primarily need to convey data. Writers in some of the humanities and in the social sciences have to communicate data too, but the distinction is broadly that data in the physical and biological sciences is quantitative (that is, relating to data, chiefly numerical), while in the humanities and social sciences there is more of a balance between quantitative and qualitative data (that is, relating to information, chiefly textual). Qualitative data often consists of quotes from interview subjects. This type of data is obviously necessary to write out in full. Quantitative data, on the other hand, absolutely requires that the author knows how to break from the flow of their text and present things visually in a table or figure. If you're coming to scientific writing with a preference or a background in qualitative data, it's important that you make this transition.

Datasets usually measure how one variable changes relative to one or several others. Common types of dataset might be a record of change over time, or at a range of physical positions, or measurements taken from individual sensor instruments/people/animals/plants/locations/replicates and so on. This means many data points will quickly accumulate, and your challenge is to be able to present this large amount of information completely and succinctly. It is simply not plausible to do this if you describe the results as a narrative account.

Data is usually presented in one of three ways: a graph, an image (these two are collectively referred to by the general term 'figures'), or in a table.

Graphs

Graphs are probably the most common type of figure. There are so many different types, each with their own best principles, that they are easy to get slightly wrong. In the upcoming sections, we'll cover all the things a good graph should include, and give advice on style and clarity to help your reader interpret it quickly and correctly.

Images

Images could be photographs, diagrams, computer models, process flow charts, or any type of simplified schematic to represent something complex. They aren't limited to presenting only data, so they can be very versatile. A close-up view of a cell taken down a microscope simply can't be converted into a graph or a table and still present the same meaningful information. The physical change in an object subjected to an experimental procedure can't usually be communicated without showing it before and after treatment. A novel method of setting up an apparatus sometimes can't be made clear without a diagram showing just how everything was arranged in the lab. When making an image, you still need to make sure it is properly annotated and presented in an appropriately formal academic style, which we'll explain throughout this chapter.

Tables

Tables are useful for presenting step-by-step information, or for presenting arrays of data, meaning lots of facts and figures where many variables are measured relative to each other at the same time. You might have analysed the chemical constituents of a large group of environmental samples, with each sample taken in triplicate. To make graphs of each chemical variable from each location would take up a huge amount of space on the page, and each graph would only contain a very small amount of information. A table format lets you set this out in an array, or a matrix, with column and row headers arranged in two neat lines to take the place of multiple graph axes repeated across your page.

Principles of data presentation

Your marker needs to be able to look at a figure or table and understand everything contained within it without referring to the main body of your text. They won't expect the figure or table to *replace* the main text, so you don't need to try to squeeze in details of why you've carried out an experiment, but your reader does need to understand what procedure was carried out and what kind of output you've chosen to show them. We'll discuss where on a page to put your figures in our section headed Positioning Tables and Figures, on p.98, but in reading all of the following advice we want you to bear in mind the principle of *ease of access*. The simpler you can make things, and the clearer you can set them out, the better the experience will be for your reader, and the higher you'll be likely to score in assessments.

Anatomy of a table

We'll deal with tables first, as they are simpler than the wide variety of items that could come under the heading of 'figure'.

Tables are used when you want to put your data into an array, or matrix, meaning a display format where each row represents one variable and each column represents another. Graphs allow you to plot one variable along the bottom and one up the side (and one into the depth axis, if you need to); tables allow you to list multiple variables in either of the two dimensions of your page simultaneously. Sometimes we're asked by students whether their data belongs in a table or a graph, and our answer often comes down to how many variables they'd like to represent at once.

With this in mind, the headings you put on your rows and columns are critical to creating an easily accessible source of information for your reader.

Here is a simple table from an investigation into self-perceptions about eating and exercise habits over the course of a day:

	Estimated calories eaten	Estimated calories burned	Estimated calorie gain/loss	Measured calories eaten	Measured calories burned	Measured calorie gain/loss
Participant 1	1900	2100	−200	2000	2300	−300
Participant 2	2500	2350	+150	2600	2400	+200
Participant 3	2050	2500	−450	2400	2250	+150

Table 9.1   A table with no organisational levels

The rows and columns are thoroughly labelled, which is good. There's a lot of repetitive text, though. Here in this next example, this has been cleaned up, and the reader's job has been made significantly easier:

	Estimated calories			Measured calories		
	Eaten	**Burned**	**Gained/lost**	**Eaten**	**Burned**	**Gained/lost**
Participant 1	1900	2100	−200	2000	2300	−300
Participant 2	2500	2350	+150	2600	2400	+200
Participant 3	2050	2500	−450	2400	2250	+150

Table 9.2   A table designed to indicate groupings or hierarchy of the study's design

A row has been added to the top of the table, and cells in that row have been merged as appropriate. It's now *immediately* clear to your marker that:

- the data is broadly divided into two sections;
- the division occurs down the middle;
- the hierarchy of titles across the top represents the way the data is grouped and then sub-grouped.

It's also worth considering the colours and fonts you use. We've put a grey background on the column headers here, and we would consider using bold font to draw the reader's attention to some parts if the table was more complex. Bold and/or italic fonts are useful for things like 'total' columns or rows at the side or the bottom of a table. Values that are of the same order of magnitude (i.e. when all values in the thousands, or in the tens of thousands, or in the hundreds) can look good aligned centrally in a column:

Force (N)
845
734
824
995

Figure 9.1 Centrally aligned numbers in a column – same order of magnitude

...but this doesn't work well when the values are of different orders of magnitude:

Force (N)
34
7.462
2561
995

Figure 9.2 Centrally aligned numbers in a column – different orders of magnitude

...as it's less easy to quickly identify the largest number, and the point of having things in a table is often to facilitate a quick scan to find the highest value, lowest value, and so on, in a set. In cases such as this, your numbers would be better justified to one side (usually the right) and expressed to the same number of decimal places so that the decimal points line up vertically:

Force (N)
34.0
7.7
2561.0
995.0

Figure 9.3   Right-aligned numbers in a column – different orders of magnitude

Anatomy of a figure

Figures include graphs and images. You'll undoubtedly have had some standard guidance about what elements need to be included in a scientific figure. We want to show you a few more elements and a few more ways to make your figures more professional, and more like figures in the published articles you'll find. Laying these things out always takes longer than you expect, so leave plenty of time for each one. It's not unusual to spend an hour or more working on a handful of graphs to make sure they each have the necessary parts, that each has the same parts as every other, and that they occupy a sensible size and position on the page.

Here's an example of a publication-quality graph:

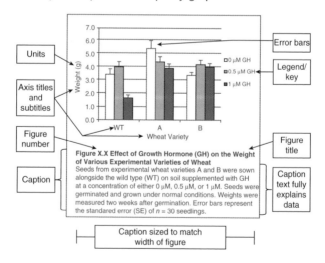

Figure 9.4   Components of a well-constructed figure (a graph)

A number on your figure is essential for helping your reader know which image to look at when you direct them to do so from the main body of your text. This raises another important point – if you never explicitly tell your reader to look at a figure, they'll keep going through the main body without stopping. Imagine yourself in such a position; since you know that figures complement what you read in the text, your attention will be squarely on that text until you have a reason to lift your eyes away and look at the complementary information.

Graphs are one type of figure; images are the other common one. Here's a publication-quality image:

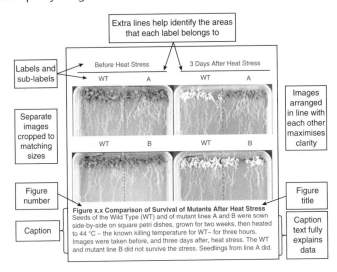

Figure 9.5   Components of a well-constructed figure (an image)

Notice how there are multiple variables expressed simultaneously in this picture: plant variety, time point, and plant condition (dead or alive). Because everything is arranged so systematically, it makes the whole story much easier for a reader to interpret. Notice, too, the way that the results are explained in the figure legend. They aren't *interpreted* – the author has stopped short of saying that one variety is able to grow successfully at higher temperatures than the other, as a conclusion this broad would require more proof than just this one experiment – but, instead, the author has simply made a few statements of the objective facts relating to one specific experiment, all of which can be supported by this one image.

Let's look at one more type of figure. Here's a micrograph (an image collected by microscope):

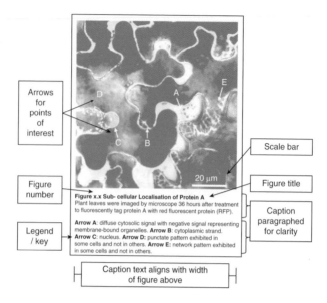

Figure 9.6   Components of a well-constructed figure (a micrograph)

Again, the figure is clear, uncluttered, simple in the number of component parts, appropriately explained with a key, and has a statement of the most important observations that the author wants to draw your attention to without interpreting them.

Colours

Colours are helpful in differentiating things like one data series from another on a graph. If you choose to use different colours, bear in mind that some of your audience will be colour-blind, and that there are different types of colour blindness. It's worth investing a little time in researching colour combinations that are 'safe' to use.

It's also worth printing your colour graphs on a black and white printer to check how this looks. If your report is to be sent to a marker electronically, they'll most likely want to print it out as it's much easier to mark a long piece of work when you can easily flick back and forth between sections. This versatility just isn't possible with an electronic document. If your marker only has access to a black and white printer, they'll need to be able to discern one data series from the next by other means. One solution is to use textures and patterns in place of colour. This works reasonably well for bar charts where you fill a 2D area, though be careful not to pack too many busy patterns next to each other into a small space. For line graphs, different patterned lines (long dashes, short dashes, dots, etc.) can be helpful. If your lines are plotted to connect discrete data points, using clearly distinguishable symbols for those points will help, too.

Here's an example:

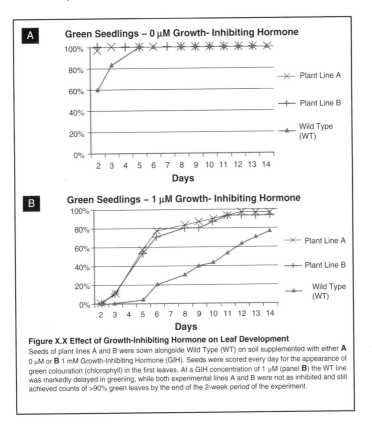

Figure X.X Effect of Growth-Inhibiting Hormone on Leaf Development
Seeds of plant lines A and B were sown alongside Wild Type (WT) on soil supplemented with either **A** 0 μM or **B** 1 mM Growth-Inhibiting Hormone (GIH). Seeds were scored every day for the appearance of green colouration (chlorophyll) in the first leaves. At a GIH concentration of 1 μM (panel **B**) the WT line was markedly delayed in greening, while both experimental lines A and B were not as inhibited and still achieved counts of >90% green leaves by the end of the 2-week period of the experiment.

Figure 9.7   Use of colours in a figure

The triangular datapoint markers, which represent the variety known as Wild Type, are perhaps the most difficult to discern (particularly in panel A). However, while they're printed here in black and white, the triangles were originally created in a colour with a much lighter shade than the other two. As this dataseries sits in front of the other two, which are represented by different cross shapes, it still stands out at timepoints where they all coincide, for example from day five onwards in panel A.

Look at some articles in the journals from your discipline for inspiration. You'll probably be surprised by how neat and compact they seem compared with the graphs you'll generate using the default options in common spreadsheet and graphing software. Simply finding ways to use less ink to represent your data goes a long way to improving clarity.

Panels

If you have multiple pieces of information to convey from one experiment, you might choose to put them all together in panels. You'll see this done in journal articles when there are many small pieces of evidence that work together to illustrate a point. If you're writing a larger piece of work, such as a dissertation covering several different topics, you might find that you want to combine several results relating to one single concept by panelling them. Be careful not to let this cause your individual images to become too small to be easily understood, though.

A typical panelling arrangement would use the individual images, graphs, and so on, to fill segments of a larger regular shape, like a square or a rectangular area on the page. Your individual data panels don't need to be of the same type; you can combine line graphs, bar charts, images, and so on, in one larger box. Each individual panel would be labelled so it can be referred to properly in the figure legend. This is usually done with a letter in the corner. For example:

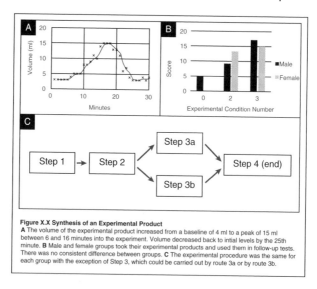

Figure X.X Synthesis of an Experimental Product
A The volume of the experimental product increased from a baseline of 4 ml to a peak of 15 ml between 6 and 16 minutes into the experiment. Volume decreased back to intial levels by the 25th minute. **B** Male and female groups took their experimental products and used them in follow-up tests. There was no consistent difference between groups. **C** The experimental procedure was the same for each group with the exception of Step 3, which could be carried out by route 3a or by route 3b.

Figure 9.8   A multi-panel figure

You needn't use letters if you'd prefer to use Roman numerals, but, whatever system you go for, make sure that it is different from the main numbering system you use to identify different figures, and also different from any system you use to mark features within the figures, such as the arrows marked by letters in Figure 9.6.

Dealing with outliers and unusual data points

You may have noticed the incomplete datasets in the graphs we used earlier to illustrate the principles of graph colouring and symbols in Figure 9.7. If you look closely at panel A, you'll notice that the trend line for plant variety B (marked by '+' symbols) had no data for days 2, 6, or 14. You'll also notice that the trend lines for neither plant variety A nor the Wild Type had any data for days 4 and 7. This brings us to the question of what to do when you have an incomplete, or unbalanced, dataset. Unbalanced datasets might also include things like population samples that include many more males than females, or many more measurements from one piece of equipment than from another.

If you were examining the difference between some measurement of one gender and the other – for example, the average lifting capacity of untrained females compared with average lifting capacity of untrained males – then it's true that your smaller sample size for males is less likely to accurately represent the true average capacity for all males worldwide, but once your data collection phase is complete, there is nothing you can do about this. You should continue with the data you have. Some students have come to us with suggestions of reducing the female data set until it matches the size of the male one. Our question in response to that is: 'On what basis will you decide which measurements to drop?'

Do you remove the outliers at each end, that is, the strongest and the weakest females, because they're the least like the average? This reduces the variability in your data, which would be akin to showing that your experiment reliably produced almost the same result each time. Do you remove only the weakest? Or only the strongest? Removing data points like this from only one end will change the average you calculate. Do you remove the females who were closest to the average, then, so that your average does not change much but your sample sizes become equal? There is still no sound scientific reason for doing this. The data you have is the data you have; your job is to dispassionately analyse it.

Certain statistical analyses you might choose to carry out will require that your datasets are organised in specific ways. Some tests may absolutely require that they contain an equal number of sample points on each side. This doesn't mean our skewed, hypothetical data set is unusable; it simply means this particular statistical test would not be appropriate. The details of different statistical tests are outside the scope of this book, but it would stand you in good stead to familiarise yourself with the most common statistical operations required for your field.

Positioning tables and figures

You won't always be able to position your figures next to the text that accompanies them. If your text ends at the bottom of a page, your figure will have to be overleaf. If your text refers to two figures simultaneously, and each figure is large, your second figure could be two pages away from the main body text that introduced it. If you put yourself in the position of a marker or a reader, you can see how frustrating it would be to repeatedly flick back and forth to compare a graph with its legend, or, even worse, scroll up and down on a screen.

That said, your figures should come as close to their introduction in the text as possible without coming before. You might choose to dedicate a section across the whole width of your page to your figures, as we've done with our examples here.

If you have a figure that is unavoidably wider than it is tall, it might be easier for your reader to interpret if you choose not to squeeze it into the space between the left and right edges of a page, thereby making it smaller and losing detail. This is particularly problematic whenever you have created a large table with many columns but only a few rows. To keep the text large enough to read, your table or figure may end up spilling off the edge of your page. Instead, consider rotating your figure or table by 90 degrees to take advantage of the greater distance between the bottom and the top of a page. This means, of course, that your reader will physically turn the page so they are looking at it in landscape orientation, so use your judgement about whether it would also make sense to rotate the text in your figure caption as well.

Different types of data, and how to present them

Staff who mark first-year reports frequently comment on the choice of graphs their students have used. The most common errors are to do with using the wrong type of graph in the first place, or using the right type of graph but misrepresenting the relationship being investigated.

Before we look at ways to represent data, let's first look at the different *types* of data.

Types of data

Categorical vs continuous

A very large part of your decision about how to represent your data will depend on whether it measures something on a sliding scale, or whether it measures something that's measured in separate categories.

Heights, weights, electrical potentials, volumes, concentrations – these are all quantities that can take any value at all between the relevant maximum or minimum for the thing being measured. Yes, we measure them with scales that are divided into steps like metres or centimetres, or volts or millivolts, but those are artificial divisions put in place by the scientists who first devised those scales. The physical quantities are not limited to only the values that our tools can distinguish. These quantities are referred to as **continuous** variables and we can plot them on certain types of axes.

Nationality, hair colour, subatomic particle type – these are all variables which can either be one thing or another. Yes, someone's nationality can be mixed, but they would either declare themselves to be predominantly one nationality, or they would declare themselves to be a mix of A, B and C, and this mixture would then be their category. Likewise, we give different names to hair colours and don't measure them along a quantitative scale, and subatomic particles must be of one type or another. **Categorical** variables like these are plotted on different types of axes.

There are other ways of breaking down continuous and categorical variables (you may have heard of terms like **ordinal** and **discrete**) but the concepts of continuous and categorical are enough for us to deal with for now.

Types of plot

In the next few subsections, we'll give you advice on how to use different ways to represent data, but one feature underpins them all: the variable you have control over – the independent variable – should go on the **X axis**, and the variable you are measuring – the dependent variable, so named because its values are dependent on whatever you're controlling in your experiment – should go on the **Y axis**. (The **Z axis** can be used to represent a second independent variable, if required).

Continuous variables against continuous variables

This section is about graphing two continuous variables against each other. Continuous variables need to be plotted on axes that are proportional to the values being plotted; in other words, for every increase in the value you want to plot, you have to move along the axis by a defined amount. The axes can be *directly* proportional, meaning, for example, that a doubling of the value you wish to plot means a doubling of the distance along the axis you must place your data point, or they can be *exponentially* proportional, meaning you will be using log or semi-log paper.

Scatter plots

When you plot continuous variables against continuous variables, you therefore need to have a continuous scale along each axis. The only type of mainstream graph that allows for this is the **scatter plot**. It allows you to choose any combination of X and Y values, and to freely plot a datapoint at their intersection.

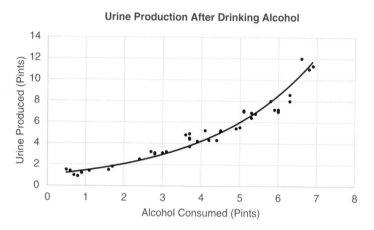

Figure 9.9   Scatter plot with free spread of dependent variable values

If you take multiple measurements at each value of your independent variable – for example, if the people represented here in Figure 9.9 had consumed *whole numbers* of pints rather than the continuous range of volumes plotted on the graph – you can still plot these all on the same set of axes, even though they may overlap. For example:

Figure 9.10   Scatter plot with values of dependent variable restricted to whole numbers, measured in triplicate

You might prefer to plot the average of your several measurements, and to this you could even add error bars as an indication of the variability of those measurements at each point:

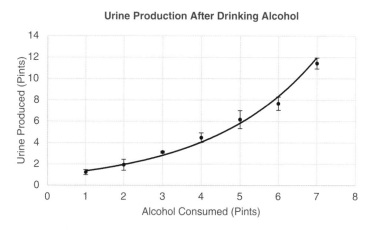

Figure 9.11   Scatter plot with dependent variable tested in triplicate, observations averaged, and plotted with error bars

The last point to make about scatter plots pertains to lines of best fit. You've probably had the debate about whether to connect your data points with straight lines, or to draw a smooth line. Then you have the question of whether a smooth line should weave smoothly and precisely through all of the points, or whether it should trace out a sort of average trend, missing out data points to do this. The answer to these questions always depends on what relationship you're trying to show.

Does it make sense that as you increase one variable, the other will increase/decrease steadily in response (for example, the higher the temperature, the faster a chemical reaction proceeds)? If so, then a line of best fit would most closely represent the truth of the situation to your reader. If you find a steady trend up until a point, and then there is a significant break in the pattern where the value of the dependent variable jumps massively, ask yourself whether this is likely to be genuine or whether it's a result of some human error or technological limitation in your instruments. A line of best fit shouldn't go through such abnormalities if they can't be explained in the real world.

A line of best fit tells your reader that you're claiming your results have some sort of predictive power. You will be able to choose any value of your independent variable on the X axis, move your eye from here up until you reach the line of best fit, then across to the Y axis, and arrive the value of the dependent variable that you would predict to find. If this notion of prediction doesn't apply to the real-world logic of your particular measurements, then a line is probably inappropriate.

You'll be able to use software to plot a line of best fit through any set of points, and it'll probably even be able to give you an equation to describe the line. Software is only as smart as the person operating the computer, though, and if you ask for a line of best fit on a dataset full of faulty observations, the line you get back will be meaningless.

Continuous variables against categorical variables

This situation is much more diverse and allows the use of many different types of graph. We'll give a quick explanation of the key features of the most popular ones.

Vertical bar/column charts

These are useful for plotting the frequency or magnitude of a categorical variable. They're fairly simple to create, which leads to their overuse and frequent misuse. It's possible to plot something like the voltage of every one of a series of batteries, or the concentration of a large series of chemical solutions, but this tells us very little.

In this graph, one set of batteries had been used to power a calculator, and one set had been used to power a motor. The capacity left in each battery after a defined period of time was measured and plotted:

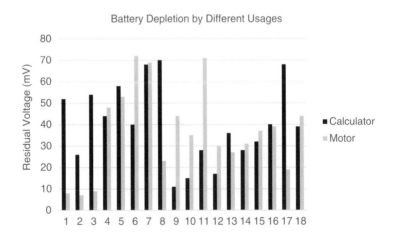

Figure 9.12   Bar chart without organisation

Instead, would it make sense to order the values from lowest to highest?

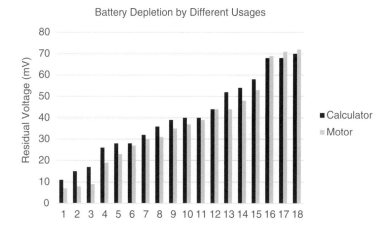

Figure 9.13   Bar chart with organisation... but still not a good graph

By enforcing order on this graph, we're suggesting to our reader that there's a connection between the order in which you test the batteries, and the voltage you'll find across them. The first battery will have around 10%, the second will have around 15%, and so on. Clearly this is not true, as the theory is just nonsense. By creating this graph, though, it's the message we're implying to our reader.

Instead, it would make much more sense to measure something like the average leftover capacity of all the batteries, or the average concentration of the solutions. Let's try to add some real-world logic here: if the batteries had all been used for the same purpose, and if the solutions had all been prepared using the same method, then we should expect to find the values of each data point in either set to be roughly equivalent. These averages can be stated quickly in the text of your report, so there's no need to create a graph for this one data point (i.e. the average).

In conclusion: make sure a bar graph would actually add something to your report about the connection between the variables on the X and Y axes before going to the effort of creating one.

Histograms

This is a specialised type of bar chart which is useful for showing how frequently different categories appear in your sample pool. In other words, for plotting a **frequency distribution**.

Imagine you wanted to see the distribution of different ages in a population. Perhaps you are only interested in ages as five-year blocks. Your graph would then look like this:

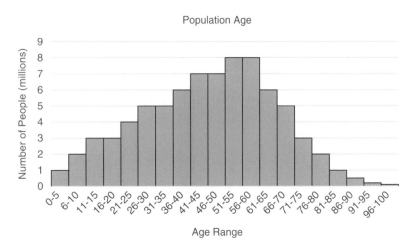

Figure 9.14 Histogram

Because you've moved away from using a continuous scale on the X axis, and instead you've given labels to the groupings, what you have is a categorical variable. The height of each bar tells you how 'popular' that category is, and the width of each bar is related to how wide the category is. In this case each category spans 5 years, and therefore each bar is the same width. The bars are also in direct contact with each other, which helps to make it clear that although each bar represents a category, these are still segments of one continuous scale.

Pie charts

We commonly see pie charts used to represent percentage data. While we completely understand the urge to do this, you should make sure to only do it if the percentages you're presenting a) are portions of the same one entity, and b) add up to 100%.

Taking the statistics from our own research on staff and student perceptions of ability in lab reports, we could say the following:

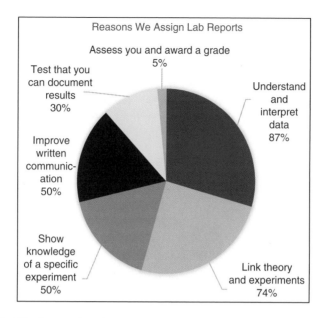

Figure 9.15   Pie chart – values do not total 100%

The percentages add up to more than 100%, so while the segments of the pie show you the relative popularity of each answer, a pie chart is not the right way to show this.

Another example. Imagine an experiment where a chemical materials were supplied to a team of students who placed them into one of two test tubes to carry out two separate reactions until all of the reactants had been used up. 100% of the materials were successfully used, and the students then measured the chemical purity of each product:

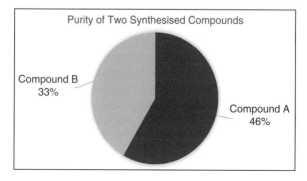

Figure 9.16   Pie chart – values not part of the same whole

The students measured something worthwhile and made a valiant attempt to present their findings, but it doesn't make sense to add together two measures of purity from two different reactions. They are portions of two separate entities, and so they are completely unrelated to each other. Instead, something like a vertical bar chart could have been used in each scenario.

Before we move on, we'll deal with another very common mistake. This mistake applies to any type of graph, but it's definitely most prevalent with pie charts.

What do you think about the distribution of answers to this question?

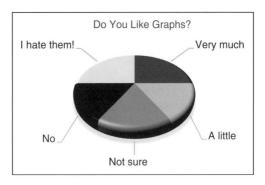

Figure 9.17 Pie chart with 3D effect

The answers seem evenly spread between the options. If we remove the 3D rotation and look at the graph face-on, however, we can see the reality is quite different.

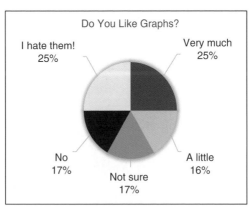

Figure 9.18 Pie chart without 3D effect

We've also included the values as part of the data labels here. We'd recommend you include both these elements in your pie charts – a flat representation, and the percentages themselves – in order to allow your reader as much chance to interpret the data correctly as possible.

Categorical variables against categorical variables

For the sake of completeness, we should mention this type of data combination. It would be possible to represent categorical variables along both the X and the Y axis, but it would be difficult to plot any relationship between these two things other than in a yes-or-no type of way, where a data point indicates a yes, and its absence indicates a no. To plot any measure of magnitude at that point would be difficult (perhaps reflected in the size of the mark made on the graph?). The easiest way to do this would be to simply replace a data point with the actual number recorded. In the end, what we have described is a table.

Types of data – summary

There are other types of graph, and many different pieces of advice we could give about combining graphs with each other to show multiple features of your dataset simultaneously. If we did, we would take up far more of this book than we have space for, but we encourage you to read voraciously on the subject of data presentation. Along with word choice and appropriate scientific tone, it is one of the major factors in determining whether your marker recognises you as someone with a confident grasp on their science, or not.

Establishing good habits with your data

There are three aspects of scientific writing that are guaranteed to take up more time than you anticipated: getting your references in place; formatting the layout of text, images, and page divisions in your final document; and tidying up your presented data. We urge you to **start early**.

If you're conducting a lengthy lab project, think about writing up your data as you go along. Not only will it help you when it comes time to write the final report, but it will give you much more chance to think about your results as you go along, and this gives you the chance to make sensible decisions about which experiments to carry out next.

One of our students said:

> Interpreting data and figures, and finding discussion points before writing the final report is really useful. When I started going through the literature to compare my results with data from other scientists, I thought of paths of investigation that I had not considered before. I kept thinking of more and more interesting experiments that would give my project higher impact.

Another said:

> I could have kept better records. It was hard to find randomly labelled data. Getting things into their final format as early as possible would have allowed me to better have an idea of the 'story' I was trying to tell, and where any gaps in my data were.

If you're collecting more data than you think you're going to present, but you don't yet know which pieces of data will make the cut, it could be helpful to have an ongoing 'journal' of your findings in the form of a PowerPoint presentation. If each slide contains one graph, or one table, it will be easy to flick through the slide deck at writing time and decide which figures will help you tell your story in the most thorough, most clear, and most logical way. This book is focused on scientific writing, but, of course, your university projects will likely involve presentations too, and having a ready-made slideshow of data will pre-empt the work you have to do at presentation-writing time.

If you're writing an essay or a literature-based dissertation, you'll want to describe the findings of others. It's perfectly permissible to use their graphical data in your work (unless you plan to publish the essay or dissertation, in which case you must ask permission from the copyright holder – usually the publisher of the journal. Be aware that 'publishing' includes the act of making a thesis available online, which more and more universities do, particularly with master's and PhD theses). Remember that the author of the article you're borrowing from had their own purpose; to tell the world about their science as fully as they could. Your purpose is to answer an essay or dissertation research question, and so you perhaps don't need to use every piece or every panel of their figure. Some of the labels, annotations, or table rows may not be relevant to your work.

In these cases, we recommend that you mask those elements so *your* reader doesn't get confused by trying to make sense of them. Overlaying them with white boxes is a quick and easy workaround. The original figure's caption is probably irrelevant to your audience too, so you should disregard it and write your own one to put the data in context with your assignment. As always, remember to cite the source in the new caption, and in the main body text where you direct your reader to look at this figure, and again in the full reference list.

In our section Principles of Data Presentation on p. 89, we showed you the most important general principles of designing and showing your figures and tables. It's important that your marker sees you can do this consistently from the start to the end of your work. Once you have decided on a style – meaning the font, the text size, whether or not to put borders around your figure legends, how to format your panel labels, and so on, – make sure that you stick to it. If you alter it in one place, make sure you alter it in all the others.

If you're using Microsoft Word, you'll save hours of your life by learning how to make use of the Styles feature. This lets you tag specific pieces of text as first-level Headings (useful for chapter titles), second-level Headings (useful for sub-section titles), third-level Headings, and so on. Once you have all of these tagged, you can quickly and easily control the style of all headings throughout your document by making one master change to the options for the appropriate Style. This is also invaluable for creating your Table of Contents. Word can auto-generate your Table of Contents, and it gathers the text for each entry by scanning through the document for everything you've tagged as a Heading. This means if a Heading moves from one page to another, the Table of Contents will dynamically update to reflect these page number changes without you having to worry about it.

The Styles feature is also invaluable for keeping track of your Figures and Tables. As we mentioned in Chapter 4 – The Dissertation, you should include a List of Figures and a separate List of Tables in longer pieces of work like final year project reports or dissertations. The Styles feature lets you assign Styles such as 'Caption' for these. You can then auto-generate your list of Tables and your List of Figures in the same way as a Table of Contents, saving you lots of time and a lot of uncertainty.

Conclusion

We hope this chapter has given you some insight into the huge range of technicalities that contribute to a well-executed presentation of data. We also hope this gives you an appreciation of why data presentation is such a good marker of a student's capabilities in scientific communication. Much of what we've said is to help your reader interpret your findings quickly, clearly, and without having to refer too much to the main body. By doing this for them, not only will your writing be appreciated by whoever reads it, but you will be much more likely to attain a higher mark in your assignments. We hope that by now you will:

- have reflected on your own experiences of reading other people's data as well as your own work from previous assignments;
- recognise the subtle design features that have made good figures easy to understand in the past;
- understand the core features required for every figure and why these are useful to a reader;
- be more aware of common mistakes, and common pitfalls encountered when using 'helpful' software to produce visuals;
- know how to relate your main text to your figures and tables;
- be able to produce visually consistent figures that give a sense of continuity and professionalism.

Being Critical

Top 3 staff comments on being critical

► Students sometimes don't notice that the results of their calculations might not be plausible; a final 'common-sense' check on results to avoid absolute reliance on method is encouraged.

► Our students should feel encouraged to disagree with something a published author has said, as long as they can explain why.

► Critical analysis is especially important in the later years of an undergraduate degree, so if students can get into this habit early, it will stand them in good stead.

Top 3 student comments on being critical

► I don't know how to critique someone's work when I'm still learning the subject myself.

► How critical am I allowed to be, and does it all have to consist of negative comments?

► How do I build criticism into the structure of my essay/dissertation/etc.?

Being critical: what, why, when, and how?

Critical analysis is something that any university lecturer will tell you is a primary skill that they hope their students develop. They might also say that it is often the distinguishing factor between an acceptable assignment and an exceptional one. Despite this emphasis, many students have never been properly told what it really means.

So, what is critical thinking?

'Criticism' is a word that usually suggests negativity when we use it in everyday life. For example, when you hear a journalist say that one politician is 'critical' of another's policy, it usually means that they've found fault with it. As a result of this, when students are asked to analyse something critically in their coursework, they often think that they've to look for problems and weaknesses. However, in higher education, 'critical thinking' does not carry this negative connotation.

In simple terms, critical thinking is a willingness to ask questions. This simplicity of this definition does not mean that students always find this an easy task. The majority of the time, the studies that you will be asked to read have been carried out and written up by professional researchers in your field. The idea of questioning their work can seem intimidating: how can you, as someone who has perhaps only been studying this subject for a few months, be expected to make a judgment on the work of a professional researcher?

In this chapter, you'll be given the essential skills you need in order to be critical of others' work in your own writing. Learning how to be critical of others' work will, in turn, give you the skills required to assess your own work rigorously – both vital abilities in undergraduate study.

In order to do this, the scientific method will first be discussed to give you some context and help you understand *why* critical analysis is important. Then, you'll be guided through a detailed breakdown of a research paper in order to let you see exactly what you should be looking for in each section, as well as the specific type of questions you can ask of it. We'll also look at different types of study, and how you should assess these. Lastly, we'll discuss how you should deal with conflicting information.

Critical analysis and the scientific method

The scientific method is a way of thinking and behaving in order to make new, reliable discoveries in a sound way. It's difficult to define because there is no single best way to do every experiment, but one of its crucial features is that science is **self-correcting**. This means that we're constantly working at the edge of understanding, and new discoveries in the future have the power to change what we understand today. This self-correction wouldn't be possible without a willingness to be critical of previous discoveries.

Many widespread beliefs have been dismissed as a result of our capacity for critical analysis. In the 18th century, it was believed that diseases were spread through the air by toxic clouds of gases called 'miasmas'. Now we know that the air itself isn't responsible, but we do have an understanding of disease transmission by direct contact, by airborne pathogens, or by disease agents transported around by vectors, like the malaria parasite carried by harmless mosquitoes. In chemistry, we once tried to turn lead into gold. A critical evaluation of the results, however, led us to update our belief about the nature of matter. In physics, light waves were proposed to travel through an invisible, intangible substance known as the 'ether' – surely a wave needs something to ripple through? – but deduction and critical thinking on the part of Michelson and Morley in the 1800s rejected that hypothesis. In a more current example, early genetics told us that each gene had instructions for making one protein: the 'central dogma' of molecular biology. Forty years later, we know things are far more complex: another success of applying a critical eye to previously accepted knowledge.

Critical analysis also means just checking that the outcome of a calculation is reasonable and logical. If you do a series of calculations that tell you the length of a table-top object is 6 metres, you've clearly made some sort of mistake.

Being critical shouldn't be thought of as a negative activity. You're not being rude by thinking critically about someone else's work – you're showing and checking that you can think for yourself.

Of course, you always need to ensure that any evidence that disproves something you thought to be true is actually a *better* piece of evidence than the old one, and this chapter will show you how to evaluate that, but don't be afraid to challenge your tutors in the spirit of academic inquiry if you find evidence that's at odds with what they tell you. You'll begin to learn through these conversations how messy the 'truth' can be, and how the professionals teaching you reconcile such differences. You will be engaging in an academic conversation, and entering an academic community.

As you've seen, critical analysis enables progress. Now, we'll give you some guidelines to get you thinking about how to do it yourself in preparation for your own writing.

The type of critical thinking that university lecturers most commonly want to see from their students is the ability to carefully analyse results, arrive at conclusions that fit the data, and think about any exceptions or caveats that should be applied in the discussions stage. You may or may not find yourself with the opportunity to design your own experiments on your course. If you do, you'll also then get the chance to demonstrate your critical thinking in the way you set up the experimental conditions, take the measurements, and, particularly in biology, use appropriate controls.

Worked example: smoking and cardiorespiratory disease

Imagine you're researching the connection between smoking and cardiorespiratory diseases. It doesn't matter whether you know anything about these topics; you'll still be able to follow this example. The only piece of jargon we'll use is the word 'cardiorespiratory', a medical term that means 'related to the heart' (cardio-) and 'related to the lungs' (-respiratory).

In this scenario, you're testing the hypothesis that males and females are affected by smoking at different ages. You contact a local hospital and ask for access to patient data relating to smokers. The hospital is small (only 300 smokers with this type of illness) and rural, so all of these patients would have been examined by the same consultant. You separate the men and the women, you group them by age, and you plot the number of patients diagnosed in each age group on a graph.

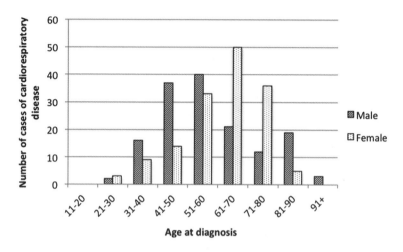

Figure 10.1   Example data from a population study

You conclude that smoking leads to a diagnosis of cardiorespiratory disease at an earlier age for men than for women.

Before we get to the critical analysis, we'll draw your attention to the noteworthy parts of the graph:

- The age bracket with the most diagnoses among men is 51–60.
- The age bracket with the most diagnoses among women is 61–70.
- No patients were diagnosed before the age of 20, and very few before 30.
- No females were diagnosed above the age of 91.
- The rate of diagnosis in men declined after the age of 61, but there was a second peak between the ages of 81–90.
- Imagine a line dividing the graph between the ages of 60 and 61. While roughly two-thirds of men are diagnosed **before** 60, two-thirds of women are diagnosed **after** 61.

Every graph you examine will be drawn for a different purpose, but to give you a starting pointer you should probably be looking for patterns or trends in the data, exceptions to trends, and/or differences in the values between the different subjects (or subject groups, as in this case).

Now that you've read about the experimental design, seen the data, and read the conclusion, *do you agree?*

First, we'll discuss the weaknesses.

Weaknesses:

- The sample size is small (300) relative to the number of smokers in the country (a justified estimate would put this in the millions for the UK).
- 'Cardiorespiratory diseases' affect the heart and the lungs, so we are probably looking at data from people with many different conditions, each of which will have different relationships with smoking.
- We don't know how long each person had been smoking: a 44-year-old on this graph may have started only three years previously, while a 38-year-old may have been smoking for two whole decades.
- These patients all came from one geographically isolated area, so perhaps they are more genetically similar to each other. Heart disease is strongly affected by genetics, so these patients may not be representative of the situation in the wider population.
- Only one hospital was involved; who knows whether they classify patients differently from other hospitals, or use a different 'checklist' for diagnosis?

As we've said, critical analysis also involves looking at strengths.

Strengths:

- People are naturally variable: two 55-year-olds may be different, while a 52-year-old and a 57-year-old may be physiologically quite similar, so grouping patients into 10-year-groups avoids creating artificial divisions for every year of age.
- The patients came from one hospital with one consultant, so we can be fairly confident they were diagnosed according to the same criteria.

Overall, the conclusion here probably does not stand up to scientific scrutiny. We have deliberately avoided any statistical analysis – that is beyond the scope of this book – but such analyses are a powerful tool for critiquing. There are also a few other minor strengths and weaknesses we've noticed, so have a think on your own. The results do, however, suggest there may be a trend worth exploring in further studies. Word choice here is key. If you were to write up this report, using qualifiers like this:

'This result *supports the hypothesis* that... though further studies with more patients must be done to prove *or disprove* this correlation beyond doubt'.

...is much better than saying:

'This result shows that...' or 'This result proves that...'

...both of which make definitive claims.

Anatomy of a research paper

Now that you've had a chance to think about how to critically assess your own work, what about other people's work? In order to understand how to critically analyse a piece of research, it is vital to understand how research papers are typically structured and what kind of information you can expect them to provide. The majority of scientific papers are written using the IMRaD model: introduction, methods, results, and discussion. Each section is expected to do a very specific job, and this means that you can ask very particular questions of each section to become familiar with the experiment. Table 10.1 gives an overview that you can use to help you do this.

Section	Purpose	Questions to ask
Abstract	This should succinctly describe what the paper is about.	Does this provide a general overview? Are there any key terms I need to understand?
Introduction	This should describe the purpose of the study, and why it is of importance. It should also provide enough context that the reader can understand the paper, and how it relates to the broader field. Any specialised terminology or concepts should be defined and explained here.	Has the writer clearly explained how the study relates to the broader field? Do I understand the purpose of the study? Do I understand the significance of this study? Do I have enough information to confidently read this paper? Are there any terms or ideas that I need to research before reading further?
Methods	This should describe, in enough detail for replication, the methods used to carry out the experiment to answer the question posed by the study.	Is everything described in specific and consistent detail? What was the sample size? What controls were used, and why?

Table 10.1 Questions to ask of each section of a research paper

Section	Purpose	Questions to ask
Results	This should present the data resulting from the experiment. It might not include every result, but will offer representative data.	What did they find in each sub-experiment?
Discussion	This presents the ideas that can be inferred from the results. Patterns, relationships, and general principles will be described. The implications of these will also be placed in a broader context. Any contradictions and exceptions should be clearly pointed out and suggestions made for how these might be resolved.	How can the specific findings of the study be more broadly understood and applied?

Table 10.1   *(Continued)*

You might initially find it difficult to read research papers and ask the necessary questions. That's understandable. Papers are often densely written, using specialised vocabulary. Take each section at a time and read it twice before you begin to ask questions. Make sure you note down your assessment of each section, with examples alongside it. Remember, as we said at the outset of this chapter, your evaluation is likely to contain positive and negative elements. When incorporating this information, think back to what was discussed in Chapter 7 about how to incorporate and reference other people's work.

The questions we've just examined establish your understanding of the paper, crucial in creating a foundation for an effective critical analysis. The next section will look at that critical analysis in detail, and consider the more specific questions you should be asking.

Valid criticisms you can make

When lecturers tell you to critique a piece of scientific work that someone else has written, it's perfectly normal to feel like you're just not qualified to do so yet. After all, you may only have done a couple of experiments, so you can't use your own experience to recognise what is good and what is bad, what will work and what won't. So, what are they expecting you to say?

This is where you take the principles of scientific rigour that you've learned and see whether you can poke any holes in the logic of the author of the work you're analysing. The most common criticisms fall into two categories: problems with how an experiment was designed and carried out (the methods), and problems with interpretation of the results.

Problems with design

Ask these questions when reading the introduction and methods sections.
    Regarding the background and justification:

- Has the author made any unfounded assumptions?
- Does the author misrepresent other pieces of research that you're aware of?
- Are pieces of research mentioned relevant and current?
- Are there studies missing that I expected to see referenced?

Regarding the methods used:

- How many replicates were used?
- Was the experiment allowed to happen for a long enough time to be able to reveal a difference between condition A and condition B?
- What controls would *you* have used? (How many variables could have affected the outcome, and was a control condition used for each? Were they carried out separately?)
- Can you think of any confounding factors not mentioned by the authors? (These would mask any genuine results. For example, you might read a study which concludes that cows fed on a certain type of new cattle feed grow to a larger size. However, if you are not told about their general living conditions you might not be able to see that, for example, they are also treated with a new antibiotic that gives a growth advantage.)

It often helps to imagine that you are a competing scientist working in the same field. You're not expected to be able to come up with a whole experimental design on your own yet, but if you can see a small shortcoming in someone else's work, then you should feel confident enough to say that in your coursework.

Problems with interpretation of results

By this stage in a report, you can stop worrying about how many replicates were used and focus on whether the authors' conclusions are supported by their data. They should avoid too much generalisation. For example, if a drug trial were carried out on 2000 subjects, of an equal gender mix, of equivalent ages, in Argentina, across all socioeconomic backgrounds, then although the sample was appropriately balanced within that country and was therefore very well-designed, it would be inappropriate to proclaim that the results are applicable globally. The drug may indeed eventually prove to be useful in sub-Saharan Africa or Western Europe, but we can't be sure until further research has shown that climate, diet, genetics related to ethnicity, and many other local variables don't affect the drug's usefulness among these populations. In short, it would be inappropriate to generalise.

The way you present data is crucial. The common perception of science is that the results gathered are so objectively measured that there can only be one way to interpret them. This is not the case. Data should be presented clearly, with appropriate labels and to appropriate scales to allow the reader to arrive at their own conclusions. If not, perhaps the authors have made an effort to hide results that are not as impressive as others.

Reproducibility is a central concept in science. If a result is based on only one or two measurements/replicates, how can we be sure the finding is real? Any such results should be treated with caution and healthy scepticism, and perhaps reported in your own writing as 'preliminary' or 'pilot' studies.

Extrapolation beyond the conditions used in an experiment can be dangerous. If you measure the products of a chemical reaction at a range of temperatures, then you will be able to plot a graph. This might show a predictable trend (e.g. a straight line on the graph, or a smooth curve). Can you then extend this prediction and continue the line beyond the temperature range you measured? Can you be sure?

Some other questions you can ask of the data and discussion sections:

- Has this section fully answered the question posed in the introduction?
- Do the data and the conclusions drawn support each other?

Some of these criticisms will be relevant to your field and some will not. The best way to familiarise yourself with the conventions of your subject is to read any papers suggested by your lecturers and, as well as learning about the findings, taking the time to read about *how* and *why* they did things the way they did.

Here's a short worked example to help you get a sense of valid criticisms you might make.

Worked example: testing the effectiveness of different stretching methods

The aim here was to measure the effectiveness of PNF (proprioceptive neuromuscular facilitation) stretching versus static stretching. The subjects were participants in exercise classes at a local gym. Participants book classes in advance, and so there was no variation in attendance over the one month duration of the experiment. Participants' flexibility was measured beforehand using the following indirect flexibility tests:

- Sit and reach test;
- Calf muscle flexibility test;
- Shoulder flexibility test.

Twenty participants at morning classes used PNF stretches in warm-up and cool-down. Twenty participants at afternoon classes used the same static stretches which were normally used in class. After one month, flexibility was measured again using the same tests. On average, participants who had used PNF stretches showed a 2.5% greater increase in flexibility in the sit and reach test over those who used static stretches, a 1.7% greater increase in the calf muscle flexibility test, and 0.9% in the shoulder flexibility test.

Valid criticisms

- Small sample size.
- No control over participants' exercise activities outside classes.
- Differing levels of innate flexibility between males and females.
- Differing levels of innate flexibility across age groups.
- Possible existence of chronic sports injuries which might affect flexibility.

Can you think of any other valid criticisms? This isn't an exhaustive list, and you may know enough about the topic to spot problems we haven't thought of.

Dealing with conflicting information

As we've mentioned, there is a perception that a properly designed scientific experiment will inevitably lead to 'the truth': a singular, reproducible outcome. However, this is not always the case and you will have to write about conflicting accounts in your academic work.

There are several reasons why authors might publish different conclusions about the same issue.

First, look at the methods. Do they differ in a small but perhaps crucial way? If so, ask yourself why they might have done things differently. There may be no reason except that they simply have different ways of working in their labs and they understandably wish to stick with those individual ways, so that they can compare tomorrow's results with the ones they gathered in that lab today, or last week, or last year. If there is a reason you *can* spot, mentioning this at the appropriate point in your academic writing will help your reader understand the science you are explaining, and will also show your marker that you are capable of critical thinking.

The most common way for students to address such discrepancies is to conclude their assignment by confidently recommending that 'further work must be done'! This is probably true, but you can easily be more sophisticated than this.

Can you identify the *type* of work to be done? Would a larger sample size help the statistical interpretation of the results? Would a better control be useful? If you've identified the difference in the papers that led to different results, can you explain exactly how the two designs could be adjusted to be compatible? The more specific you can be, the better your analysis will read.

Hierarchies of evidence

In Chapter 7, we discussed evaluation of different sources. We told you to pay attention to the recency of your information, the expertise of the person who provided it, and we described the peer-review system. In Chapter 9, we looked at the principles of data presentation. You might have checked off all of these concerns and satisfied yourself that your source is reputable. However, not all scientific papers are created equal.

Reports can be written about various individual stages of research from primary lab experiments through to finished, real-world application. Each piece of research aims to answer a question, and the reality of scientific work is that the research might be quite distantly removed from the real-world scenario 'in the wild'. The more closely a piece of research can simulate that realistic situation, or the more closely an experimental treatment can be delivered to the end-user (e.g. it's more instructive to test drugs on a small group of people than on cells grown in a Petri dish), the better. However, early research is often carried out in situations far removed from the real scenario, for a huge number of reasons. This doesn't mean the research is bad, but it means you need to be aware of its strengths and its limitations.

This section will very briefly introduce you to the common essential features of different types of scientific study, and will rank them in a loose hierarchy according to how widely their results could reasonably be applied. The tables of strengths and weaknesses will help you think about whether a study was designed appropriately for the situation, and whether the author's conclusions are possible to make given the limitations of the methodology.

Lab research (applicable to biology, chemistry, physics)

Experiments in a lab are able to be well-designed to include control conditions so that only one variable is measured at a time. One major drawback is that by controlling all but one factor, the researcher can rarely reliably reproduce the varied conditions encountered in the wild. Table 10.2 summarises its main strengths and weaknesses.

Lab research	
Strengths	**Weaknesses**
• Possible to measure the effect of only one variable at a time • Conditions can be precisely controlled	• Tightly controlled conditions may not represent reality

Table 10.2   Lab research – strengths and weaknesses

A food crop grown in a laboratory growth room with its constant temperature, humidity, and light intensity is useful for measuring the impact of a new genetic mutation on food yields, but will things be the same in the messiness of the great outdoors? Human beings can't be confined in rooms and told exactly how to behave for very long, so how can we carry out investigations on people? To answer this, we need to move on to one of the observational study types described below.

Medical, veterinary, and other health-related research: observational studies

The studies under this subheading are all carried out with little or no intervention by the researcher and are thus referred to as 'observational' studies. Table 10.3 provides a brief overview.

Case study/case report/case series	
• Written when new symptoms are found, or are found together in a new combination • Only describe one or a very small number of individuals	
Strengths	**Weaknesses**
• Crucial for tracking the emergence of new diseases or identifying causes of symptoms/side-effects	• Contain only one, or a few, data points • Unlikely to prove causal relationships without further studies
Cross-sectional study	
• A report on many individuals at the same time – a 'cross-section' of the population	

Table 10.3   Observational study types – strengths and weaknesses

Strengths	Weaknesses
• Allows for sample sizes from tens up to tens of thousands • Individual variations more likely to be averaged out • Can be relatively cheap, especially if questionnaire-based	• Only provides a snapshot • Cannot follow progression of a situation • Difficult to establish causal relationships • Questionnaires rely on honesty, correct memory, and many other factors

Case-control study

• Designed to identify an unknown cause of a condition
• Subjects recruited and split into two groups – those with the condition (cases) and those without (controls)
• Researchers examine everyone's history to look for something common in the history of the case subjects that was not in the history of the controls, or vice versa

Strengths	Weaknesses
• Large sample size makes results more reliable • Case group allows the creation of a list of possible causes • Control group allows the creation of a list of factors that can be discounted	• Difficult to definitively prove causal relationships beyond doubt • Retrospective nature means results are subject to recall ability of subjects

Cohort study

• Similarly to case-control study, this looks for a connection between an exposure and an outcome in a population
• Unlike a case-control study, the exposure and outcome are usually known. The aim is to more fully understand how the exposure leads to the outcome by following over time
• This is the first long-term study in this list – referred to as a 'longitudinal' design
• Can investigate how an existing outcome has developed ('retrospective') or how a recent exposure is connected with an expected outcome in the future ('prospective')

Strengths	Weaknesses
• Large sample size makes results more reliable • Long-term nature allows for study of many details, increasing reliability of any causal relationships discovered	• Retrospective versions are subject to recall ability of subjects • Prospective versions can cause alterations in participant behaviour due to awareness of being monitored

Table 10.3   *(Continued)*

Medical, veterinary, and other health-related research: experimental studies

These studies allow a researcher to dictate what should or should not happen. Since they can test a hypothesis by controlling some variables, we refer to these studies as following an 'experimental' methodology rather than an observational one. Table 10.4 shows some of their strengths and weaknesses.

Randomised controlled trials (RCTs)	
• 'Trial' means a test of a hypothesis, e.g. 'drug X will alleviate symptoms of disease Y' • 'Control' is used in the usual scientific sense: variables can be *controlled* (duration, intensity) as well as controlled *for* (using positive and negative control conditions) • 'Randomised' means subjects are assigned to a group in a random way – ensures a mix of ages, gender, etc. and reduces experimental bias • Usually built on previous findings; allows predictions to be made	
Strengths	**Weaknesses**
• Widely referred to as the 'gold standard' in establishing causal relationships because so much can be controlled by the researcher • Knowing exactly what is being tested means participants can be excluded if it's clear they would not respond in a standard way, e.g. if they have a second, related condition • 'Blinding' means subjects don't know whether their treatment should have an effect – eliminates participant bias • 'Double-blinding' means researchers working with the subjects also do not know which treatment they are giving, eliminating bias	• Inappropriate randomisation can lead to bias (e.g. allocating to groups by year of birth is not truly random and can lead to groupings of people with much in common)

Table 10.4 Intervention study types – strengths and weaknesses

Applicable to all types of science: reviews, meta-analyses, and systematic reviews

The study types described in the previous sections are examples of primary research, where an investigation is carried out to produce results. Reviews and meta-analyses are based on the findings published in these primary research papers.

- Reviews summarise tens or hundreds of other papers for easy reading.
- Meta-analyses take the findings of primary research papers, combine them, and produce an extra statistical analysis based on this larger dataset.
- Systematic reviews are like reviews, but the authors go through a very specific series of steps when looking at each paper (they apply a 'system').

It is important for you to know that these exist, but it's unlikely that you'll carry out any critical analysis on publications at this level in your early years of study. As a newcomer to scientific writing, you will probably use reviews to guide you into a new field, but we want to keep the focus of your critical analysis first on primary research papers.

Conclusion

Hopefully, we have convinced you that refinement of previous knowledge is essential to the development of science. Now that you have the tools required to perform a critical analysis, you should not be afraid to make educated suggestions for improvement, regardless of your practical experience.

Making these types of critical judgements now will undoubtedly align with the higher sections of your university's grading scheme and lead to better marks in your assignments, but it will also prepare you for when you eventually have to read the scientific literature, decide what you want to find out, and design appropriate experiments to tackle those questions yourself.

Now that we've tackled all aspects of the linked processes of reading and analysis, and you've carried out your reading and taken all the necessary notes, the next section of the book will deal with beginning to write your first draft.

Part

3

Getting Down to Writing

Producing a Draft and Building Your Argument

Top 3 staff comments on structure:

► Students often don't stop to consider whether their answers are sensible.
► I'm not sure what conclusion the student came to after describing all these pieces of information.
► Paragraphing is often erratic.

Top 3 student comments on structure:

► It's hard to know where to begin with it. I write what I know first and the structure sort of develops from that.
► I don't understand how to get my writing to flow.
► I don't have time to think about structure before I write.

Getting ready to write

You've selected your question and deconstructed it, looking for command words and limiting factors. You've searched the library for resources. You've decided which resources are most relevant, and you've analysed them. You've taken all the notes you need. You've considered how your work relates to the wider literature. The good news is that you have already made a substantial start on writing, since the mental process of writing is, by this point, well underway. This chapter will take this further, into the production of your first draft.

From our experience, we've found that science students sometimes lack confidence in their writing abilities. This is often because writing was part of subjects that they didn't enjoy at school. Consequently, this made them find writing boring or difficult. This can sometimes leave students with the impression that they are 'bad' at writing.

It might surprise you to learn that having worked with students from all disciplines, our experience is that science students' writing skills are on a par with their fellow students in the arts and social sciences. In fact, they're usually slightly better. Based on this, we'd like to ask you to set aside any residual anxieties you have over writing, and consider university writing as an entirely new skillset.

As well as asking you to start your time at university fresh in terms of your attitude towards writing, and your beliefs about your skills as a writer, we'd also like to suggest that you adopt a new way of writing which will help you to avoid many of the common pitfalls first-year students encounter. This method will also help you to develop a relaxed, personalised writing method and enable you to become comfortable with writing, and to feel confident in your work.

Drafting

You've probably had teachers advise you in the past to produce several drafts of written work. This often isn't very popular advice. Producing several drafts sounds time-consuming and laborious. Instead, many students prefer the idea of writing one draft, your best effort, which is then edited repeatedly.

This sounds like it will save you time and work, but it will ultimately cost you more time and stress. Trying to make everything perfect first time leads to hours spent revising one section, one paragraph, one sentence. This eats into your study timetable, creating anxiety about the deadline.

Although you might think that your tutors produce effortlessly fantastic first drafts, this is rarely the case. First drafts look messy, and nothing like their final version. In fact, your tutors' first drafts will look a lot like yours. There might be missing words, or lack of precision in word choice. There might be a lot of repetition. The structure itself can look untidy, leaping between ideas without links, with some paragraphs too long, and others too short. There might be gaps where they have to check facts. Often, after reading the first draft, it becomes apparent that it begins by saying one thing, and ends by saying another, or that the central question hasn't been addressed as fully or directly as it ought to have been.

There's a good reason for this disorganisation. The first draft we produce is not really about communicating our ideas to a reader.

Instead, it's where we work out our thoughts on paper. It's like showing your working for a calculation, with all the mistakes and false starts on the page. It's not really about explaining your ideas to someone else so much as it's about getting your own ideas straight, and figuring out what you do know, and what you don't know. In composition studies, the production of this type of draft is described as 'writing as a way of knowing' (McCrimmon, 1984).

The first few drafts, then, serve an important purpose. They're part of the learning process as much as note-taking. Writing drafts improves your understanding of the topic, allowing you to think carefully about how ideas are connected, and to pick up on any weak points in your understanding. This improved understanding results in a focused and comprehensive piece of work.

However, students still avoid redrafting, and stress themselves by treating this first draft as *the* draft, the one that their tutor marks, and which will affect their grade. This is an incredibly difficult and time-consuming task for them to set themselves, no matter their level of writing ability. They are taking an early draft, which is really about the writer figuring out their thoughts, and trying to edit it to make it do a completely different job: communicating information to the reader.

You will produce better work more efficiently, and make writing a less stressful experience, if you adopt redrafting as part of your writing process, and if you take on board the idea of two completely separate species of draft: a process draft, and a product draft (Murray, 1972).

Process and product drafts

Have a look at the table below.

Process draft	Product draft
Record of thinking	Presentation of ideas
Disorganised	Well-structured
Writer-focused	Reader-focused
Missing or 'wrong' words	Precise word choice
Repetitive	Concise
Uncertain	Confident
'Gappy'	Comprehensive
Thinking	Telling

Table 11.1   Process vs product draft

The first drafts you write are process drafts. They are a record of your understanding and thinking, not the finished product to be submitted for assessment. Because you know that this draft isn't going to be submitted, you won't agonise over details, which is what slows the writing process down. You can expect your writing at this point to look a lot like the draft described on the left side of the table.

Once you begin to allow yourself to think about the first draft as a process draft, a draft that gives you a space to sort out your ideas without being worried about being graded, you're less likely to feel stressed about it looking disorganised, which in turn makes it easier to write. It's okay for a process draft to look untidy, because it's for your eyes only, and you can restructure things later. It can contain grammatical errors, because you can correct these later. The process draft might reveal gaps in your knowledge, which mean that you have to do some extra revision, but this is helpful, and part of the 'process' of the process draft.

The product draft benefits from all the hard work of the process drafts. After writing the process drafts, you should be left with a clear idea of exactly what you want to communicate to your reader, the best structure for doing that, and exactly which pieces of information you want to present. In the product draft, your mind is then free to focus on your reader, thinking about the best way to clearly communicate your work.

Look at these example paragraphs. One is from a process draft, the other from a product draft in progress. The notes in bold give early indications of how the writer might want to redraft and alter their approach for the product draft.

Process paragraph

(Need introductory sentence?) Neurons are each made up of a soma, an axon, and dendrites (Bear et al., 2016). There are lots of neurons that do specific jobs: sensory neurons, interneurons, and **(check this)**. They have different structures **(check proper word for this)**: bipolar, multi-polar, and pseudo-unipolar. Neurons send and process information via chemical and electrical signalling. This is known as neurotransmission, which is enabled by ion channels which allow charged ions to flow **(transmit?)** across the cell membrane. Post synaptic neurons play a role **(does this fit here? Needs more explanation)**.

(Adapted from Bear et al., 2016).

Box 11.1   Sample process paragraph

Product draft

(Introductory sentence added) Neurons are the main component of the central nervous system (Bear et al., 2016). They are each composed of a soma, an axon, and dendrites. There are specialised types **(language now more formal)** of neurons that do specific jobs: sensory neurons, interneurons, and motor neurons. They can also be subdivided by morphology **(found the proper term for this)**: bipolar, multi-polar, and pseudo-unipolar. Neurons send and process information via chemical and electrical signalling. This is known as neurotransmission, which is enabled by ion channels which allow charged ions to flow **(rephrased to make this clearer)** across the cell membrane.

(Adapted from Bear et al., 2016).

Box 11.2   Sample product paragraph

Now that you have an understanding of these different types of draft, and how they work, we'll look in more detail about how you actually go about making them part of your writing process. Before that, though, let's think a little more about how you write in general.

Developing your own writing practice: when, where, and for how long?

Time-management is an important part of dealing with academic life. Now you have an understanding of how redrafting will actually save you time, we can look at using that writing time even more effectively. One of the methods discussed later in this chapter will help you get a clear picture of how much time you need to set aside for writing, but it's equally important to think about how to make the writing process comfortable and productive. This is an opportunity to figure out what works for you.

How long?

First of all, let's look at the length of time you spend writing. Try setting aside a couple of hours to devote yourself to the task. Pay attention to how productive you are during this time. Pay attention to how much time you spend actually concentrating on your task. Did this approach work for you? Did you find that setting aside a long period of time helped you to focus or did your attention wander frequently, meaning that you spent much less time writing than you set aside? There's no right or wrong answer.

If setting aside hours at a time didn't work for you, then you might find that you work better in short bursts. Working in 10 or 15-minute blocks throughout the day can be an effective way to get a surprising amount of writing done. Don't think that you have to sit in the library for hours on end if this approach simply doesn't work for you, and don't feel guilty if this is the case. Instead, make the most of the time between classes, or spent commuting. This approach might also be effective if you have other commitments which make it difficult for you to set aside several hours at a time, such as family or caring commitments, or part-time work. To help you use your time more effectively across the board, which will have an impact on writing time, you should look at Palgrave's pocket guide on time management (Williams, Reid, 2011).

When?

Time of day can be important, and is very individual. Some people prefer to work in the mornings, finding it difficult to motivate themselves in the afternoons. Others like to get up early, and get their writing done before the day's routine begins. Auden wrote in long blocks from 6am to 12pm, and then all afternoon until 6pm. Darwin tended to write in short bursts at 7am, then at mid-morning, and then wrote from 9pm until around midnight. I'm writing this at 11.30pm, because I like to write late at night. As long as you can make it work practically within your timetable, try to take advantage of the times of day when you are most productive.

Where?

Think about your surroundings. Where do you find it comfortable to work? Do you find it motivating to work in the library, with lots of other students around? Or do you find that distracting, and prefer to work alone at home? Do you need silence, or do you like to listen to music? There's no right or wrong answer here, everyone works differently. There's even variation within each of these choices. For example, some people might like listening to music, but find that music with lyrics is distracting when they're trying to write. Others might listen to the same song repeatedly (one student once told me he listened to the same song on repeat for four hours while writing a chapter of his PhD). Again, it's about finding whatever helps you concentrate and makes you more productive.

Managing the task

If you've identified the time and location that works for you, but you're still finding it difficult to start, then think about breaking the task down into manageable chunks. Which part of the assignment do you feel ready to tackle first? You do not necessarily have to write in order. If you would prefer to write your methods section first, as many people do, then you should feel free to do so. Sometimes just seeing words on the page can get you past that initial hurdle and motivate you to keep going.

Rowena Murray talks about two different ways of approaching writing: 'binge' writing, and 'snack' writing (Murray, 2011). While binge writing involves working for long periods of time, snack writing involves working in short bursts with a clearly defined goal:

1 Set aside a specific length of time for your writing session (20 minutes, for example).
2 Define your goal – 'I want to write a first draft of my methods section'.
3 Try to write without stopping, or going back to check what you've written.
4 Make sure you stop at the time limit.
5 Try and repeat regularly, establishing a writing habit.

This technique has the following advantages:

- Breaking your time down into blocks makes your task more manageable.
- Recording your progress lets you see that you are moving forward, and motivates you to do more.
- Taking regular breaks will help you stay rested and focused.
- Importantly, keeping track of your word count will give you a realistic idea of how much you can write in a given length of time. This will allow you to set targets in order to meet deadlines, and allow you to manage your time more effectively.

If you want to benefit even more from this approach, then try reflecting on how each block felt, as well as what you achieved. Did your attention wander at any point? Did your progress stall? Ask yourself why. Could it be that there's a concept that you're unsure about, and which requires extra revision? Are you working somewhere distracting? Is late afternoon an unproductive time for you? These are valuable observations that you can use and address in order to get past roadblocks in your current assignment and strengthen your work.

You can also use these observations to improve your writing in the long term. Knowing, for example, that you are a more productive writer when you work in the afternoon will help you manage your time more effectively by allowing you to set aside the best time to write. Try to build up a picture of the environment and style that lets you approach writing in a calm and relaxed way, and create this whenever when you have work to do.

Writing your process draft

Now that you've had some time to think about your writing habits, and how an awareness of them will make writing more productive, let's look in more detail at the process and product drafts we outlined earlier.

The process draft, as has been discussed, is a free space for you to write without worrying about someone else reading it. As such, it is difficult to give an example of how it 'should' look, as it will look different for everyone. However, these instructions will give you a sense of how this type of draft works, and let you get started. As you get more used to writing this way, you can make your own tweaks and refinements to the method.

Process draft guidelines

1 Make sure you've got the question written down.
2 You can work from a plan if you choose. This might be a more detailed plan with headings that you can write beneath, or something looser. Alternatively, you might simply want to start writing down information relating to the question.
3 Don't worry if there are gaps in knowledge, or you can't find exactly the right word to describe something: remember, no-one but you will see this version. Move on to the next sentence, or the next paragraph, if you prefer.

If you are writing the first process draft:

1 Resist the urge to go back and make small changes to sentences and paragraphs as you write. You can do that in the redrafting stages. For the initial draft, aim to get words on the page. Editing as you write will slow you down enormously.
2 If, when writing, you discover that there's a gap in your knowledge, note this, but move past it and write the next stage. The gap can be addressed later when you redraft.
3 If English is your second language, and you need to write a word in your first language, this is fine. You can check for an appropriate translation later.
4 If you've chosen to work from a plan, don't panic if you start to deviate from this. The need to deviate might point to the need to rethink your initial structure.
5 If you're finding it difficult to stop yourself tinkering with what you've written, then set yourself a time limit. Knowing that you only have 20 minutes to write will make you reluctant to go back and change things as you write.

Once you have produced your first process draft, read it carefully. Translating your ideas and knowledge from your mind to the page often helps you get a better grasp of your work, and what you want to say.

1 Look for any gaps. Do you need to do some more reading?
2 Look for repetition. Does the same information appear in different paragraphs? This might point to a structural issue.

3 Look for the parts where you had difficulty describing a process, or had difficulty discussing how ideas related to each other. Trying to choose the right descriptive words can sometimes help us more fully understand concepts and processes, or reveal where we need to reinforce our understanding.

4 Are there parts where the structure broke down? If you're writing an essay, that might mean a new structure which better reflects your approach to the question might be appropriate. If you're writing a report, then make sure you understand what kind of information needs to go in each section.

Don't feel that this means your initial research was unsuccessful. On the contrary, this means that your process draft *was* successful. Writing is a recursive process – which means that you can go back and repeat stages. You choose a question, conduct research, take notes, make a plan, produce a number of drafts, and then produce a final draft. However, you can – at any stage – go back and repeat a stage in this process. This will only strengthen your understanding and improve the quality of the end product.

After redrafting, when you have a better grasp of what you want to say, you can begin to write with an eye to the next stage: the product draft.

Writing your product draft

Sadly, you can't simply transfer your knowledge and ideas wholesale from your brain to your reader's brain. Instead, you have to communicate this through writing. Since reading is an act of interpretation, this presents difficulties. If the process draft is about you, the writer, getting to grips with your ideas, then the product draft is all about ensuring that you communicate these ideas to your reader. The key question to ask yourself is: how can I make my reader's life as easy as possible? To do this, you have to shift your thinking from a writer's mindset to a reader's mindset. Which structure is easiest to follow? Which sentence structure is clearest? Which word precisely summarises this process?

We'll go into how to achieve this in more detail later, looking at structure, punctuation, and tone, but the main ideas to take on board just now are as follows:

Product draft guidelines

Content

Your work should respond to the question in a thorough and detailed way. No matter whether you are working on an essay, report, or dissertation, ask yourself the following questions:

1 Does the reader have all the information they need in order to follow your work?

2 Have you defined important pieces of terminology?

3 Have you placed your work in a wider context (referred to appropriate literature)?

4 Are there any details/facts/theories that you are still unclear on? If you don't understand them, then you won't be able to communicate them clearly or convincingly to your reader.

5 Is everything relevant to the question? Additional information might seem interesting, but it can obscure your structure, and make your work seem cluttered. It can also imply that you were unable to identify the information that was most appropriate in order to answer the set question.

Structure

Clear structure is important at every level of your writing. Ask yourself the following questions:

1 If you are writing a lab report, then you need to ensure that each section contains the appropriate information, and that it doesn't wander from one section to another. If you are unclear on what should be contained in each section, then re-read Chapter 4. There will also be a checklist on this later in this chapter.

2 Within each section, every paragraph should be clearly structured. Each should deal with one key point. You should be able to summarise the paragraph's purpose in one sentence.

3 There should also be a logical progression within each paragraph, whether you're describing a process, or you're leading your reader through a point in your discussion, or you're building a detailed description. Disparate pieces of information tacked together do not make a paragraph.

4 Within your paragraphs, sentence structure is important. Clear, concise sentences are the most effective way to convey information. This is the case even when the information is very complex and detailed. In fact, it is especially important when conveying difficult information to make sure that your reader isn't distracted by overly long and complicated sentence structure. Think about how much information the reader can take in. Don't pile important concepts and observations on top of each other in long sentences. Not only will you fatigue the reader, but your ideas will not get the attention they deserve.

Tone

Lapses in tone are jarring, and distract the reader from your content. They can also damage your credibility. Academic writing is a demonstration of your ability to write like a professional in your field. Informal language can make it appear as if your understanding of the content is flawed, or simplistic.

1 Use of subjective language, even if it is inadvertent, can make the reader question your argument.
2 Look out for colloquialisms.
3 Try to ensure that you write in the passive voice.
4 Aim for precision (being specific) and accuracy (being correct) in word choice. Vagueness or incorrect word choice damages the overall tone of your work.

The ability to communicate yourself in writing is a vital skill in your undergraduate science degree. It will continue to be important in the workplace, and if you go on to postgraduate study and research, it will become even more important. As such, it should be something that you feel confident about. We want to encourage you to take ownership of the writing process through the techniques we discussed above. Personalise it. Realise that the redrafting process gives you control over your writing. See yourself as a writer.

Refining your structure and clarifying your argument

When writing your product drafts, it's crucial to consider how your writing can best be structured in order to enable you to communicate clearly with your reader. This requires an understanding of how to build and sustain strong structure within a piece of written work. We will look now at different methods of paragraph building, suggesting which might be especially suitable for certain purposes. We'll also demonstrate here how to maintain flow and coherence through use of signposting.

It is important to be fully aware, and understand the purpose, of the structural conventions of the work you have been assigned, whether it is a report, essay, or dissertation. We discussed, in Chapters 2, 3, and 4 and how and why each of these types of assignment differ in their structures. We also talked about what you need to understand about their structures in order to write successfully in any of these formats, and how the response that is expected of you helps to define your structure. If you are still uncertain about this, then you should reread either Chapter 2, 3, or 4 (depending on which assignment type you have been set) before proceeding.

However, as well as format-specific guidelines, there are also structural techniques which can be used across all of these assignment types in order to help to facilitate a logical flow in your writing. A knowledge of these techniques will give you the power to create strong, coherent pieces of work which effectively showcase your knowledge and understanding. We'll look at how to achieve this by examining a range of paragraphing techniques, and suggesting different strategies that will ensure you maintain a flow throughout the whole piece of work.

As mentioned, earlier chapters which dealt with analysing the question, gathering the necessary resources, and reading critically, demonstrated to you how a plan for structure should evolve naturally from your research. This early plan is the plan that you should have in mind and keep by your side as a guide when you write your initial process draft. However, you shouldn't allow adherence to it to slow down your writing. If, as you are writing, you find that things start to flow in a different direction, and you begin to deviate from your plan, you should allow this to happen. This could mean that you have opened up a new avenue of enquiry, or that your initial plan perhaps needs revision. This is a positive thing, and the whole purpose of carrying out the process draft.

This might happen a few more times as you write your process drafts. It's a good example of the idea of 'writing as knowing', the act of writing as a means of sorting your thoughts out on the page. This is why it's important that you take the time to produce multiple drafts. Your final product will be much stronger after you have investigated every avenue of your thinking, and figured out which ideas are strong, and deserve to be emphasised, and which are irrelevant, and can be safely excised. Once you have produced a draft that represents your thoughts on the topic, and you know exactly what you want to communicate to your reader, then it's time to think about the best ways to structure the work to make sure your reader can fully follow your points.

Paragraphing

First of all, let's think about paragraphs, and what they actually do.

Most students, at every level from first year to postgraduate researcher, home and international, have asked us both exactly the same question about paragraphs: how long should a paragraph be? This question comes from not really understanding what a paragraph is for. The simplest definition of a paragraph is that it is a section of text which looks at one point within your wider discussion. As such, there is no set answer to this question, although very long or very short paragraphs might point to wider structural issues, which will be discussed later in the chapter. Instead, it is more productive to think about what role a paragraph plays in your written work.

Basic principles

No matter the particular type of paragraph that is being written, no matter the discipline, to do its job effectively, every paragraph has to be focused, coherent, and fully developed.

Focused

A paragraph should cover one main point.

Coherent

A paragraph should have some sort of 'flow' throughout. It should not read as a random chunk of information.

Fully developed

It's important that ideas and concepts discussed in paragraphs are fully explained and backed up with evidence when appropriate. It's easy to forget to do this, especially if the writer thinks that the data is so obvious that no explanation is required, or that a statement does not require explanation.

In the next section, we'll look at the most common paragraph problems that we tend to see in students' writing, why these happen, and how to avoid them.

Common paragraph problems

The point you have chosen to cover is too broad for one paragraph

If this happens, you will find that although your paragraph technically deals with one main point, it still lacks unity, because there are too many subsidiary ideas that can be explored under the umbrella topic. On top of that, these subsidiary ideas are unlikely to be fully developed, because they're all fighting for attention within one paragraph. Structurally, the paragraph will also start to look untidy, because you are trying to deal with too many ideas at once, and there are threads of discussion spiralling off in different directions. As a whole, the paragraph is likely to be very long, have a jumbled structure, and exhibit a lack of properly developed ideas.

> Attempting to understand how the brain deals with music is complex. The frontal areas of the brain seem to be involved when music elicits an emotional response (Warren, 2008). The brains of musicians and non-musicians seem to deal with musical input differently. Parts of the brain which deal with issues such as motor tasks seem to exhibit structural changes. There are similarities in how the brain deals with music and how it deals with language. For example, Broca's area is implicated in both. Rhythm and tonality both involve complex processes crossing several different structures. When the rhythm is particularly complex, even more parts of the brain become involved, such as the cerebellum. Damage to the amygdala can affect the emotional perception of music, according to a study carried out by Gosselin, Peretz, Johnsen and Adolphs in 2007. Brain damage can impact on musical ability, depending on the part of the brain which is affected, and the role it performs in terms of musical ability.
>
> (Adapted from Warren, 2008).

Box 11.3   Paragraph with too many controlling ideas

It's not easy to follow, is it? It's unpleasant to read because of the burden that is being placed upon the reader, with far too many large ideas to deal with at once. You will also notice that while there are some connections drawn between ideas (damage to the amygdala and generalised damage), the writer flits distractedly from one idea to the next as it occurs to them.

This type of paragraph can be especially frustrating for a marker to encounter. In Part One: Understanding Different Types of Scientific Writing, we discussed the various reasons why markers set specific types of assignments and questions. In this kind of paragraph, your marker can see that you broadly understand the topic and all its implications, but because you've crammed so much information into one section, you have only given yourself enough space to touch on each issue. As such, they can't get a full sense of the depth of your understanding and analysis, and can only grade and assess you on what you've offered, which is truncated and jumbled.

The solution

Look carefully at the topic sentence. Would it be possible to break this down into smaller points? If you find this difficult, then look at the subsidiary ideas fighting for attention in the body of the paragraph. Would these three or four smaller points actually be better as paragraphs in their own right? There will still be a broader sense of coherence in your essay/report, because all these points are connected, but now each will have space to be properly expanded and developed. As such, your marker will now also be able to get an idea of the depth of your understanding.

In the example here, the obvious solution is to abandon the very broad, and to then look and see whether the ideas raised in the paragraph could be grouped into conceptual categories. So, from that paragraph, you might be able to create the following paragraph plan:

Structures involved in processing music
↓
Musicians vs non musicians – structural differences
↓
How damage can impact musical ability
↓
Specific case study – the amygdala.

Box 11.4 Example of a basic paragraph plan

Now, from one overly long and confusing paragraph, you have created a four paragraph plan which your marker will be able to follow and, within which, you will be much better able to expand and add detail to your discussion, thus demonstrating your knowledge and understanding through your writing.

The point you have chosen to cover is too narrow

If this happens, you might find that your essay/report/dissertation contains lots of very short paragraphs. The paragraph is unified, and coherent in itself, but it needs to be set in a broader context in order to be meaningful and relate to the main question. When we encounter this in students' writing, what we often see is a pattern throughout the whole work of a complete paragraph, followed by a much smaller paragraph which seems to have been cut adrift.

> One of the reasons that smell, memory, and emotion seem to be connected has to do with the structure of the brain (Wilson and Stevenson, 2003). The amygdala, which is involved in processing memories to do with emotions such as fear and anger, plays an important role. It is located close to the primary olfactory complex, which deals with olfaction. The amygdala has direct connections to the hippocampus, which deals with short and long-term memory. It can be seen to be important, for survival reasons, that mammals develop and store memories to do with fear and anger.
>
> The primary olfactory complex, amygdala, and hippocampus are all part of the limbic system, although the concept of the limbic system is contested by some neuroscientists (Heimer et al., 2007).
>
> (Adapted from Wilson and Stevenson, 2003; Heimer et al., 2007).

Box 11.5   Example of incomplete paragraph

Can you see how that very small paragraph should actually be reabsorbed by the main paragraph? The writer has perhaps felt that this piece of information was too much of a departure from the rest of the paragraph. However, it's not really enough to stand as a paragraph on its own. Besides, the information that the olfactory complex, hippocampus, and amygdala are all part of something known as the limbic system would seem to be important background information for this paragraph.

This type of paragraph will disrupt the structure of your work. Each point might be well-developed, but lots of small, disconnected paragraphs will ultimately have an impact on the overall coherence and structural tightness of the essay/report/dissertation, making it seem 'choppy' and awkward to read. The fact that there are several smaller points disconnected from their wider context might lead your marker to conclude that you don't understand how to contextualise and synthesise this information, and thus give them an inaccurate picture of your abilities.

The way to correct this issue is to think carefully about how the information can be reabsorbed into the main paragraph, and then restructured. Consider the following redraft:

One of the reasons that smell, memory, and emotion seem to be connected has to do with the structure of the brain (Wilson and Stevenson, 2003). The amygdala, olfactory complex, and hippocampus are all part of a larger structure known as the limbic system. The amygdala, which is involved in processing memories to do with emotions such as fear and anger, plays an important role. It is located close to the primary olfactory complex, which deals with olfaction. The amygdala has direct connections to the hippocampus, which deals with short and long-term memory. It can be seen to be important, for survival reasons, that mammals develop and store memories to do with fear and anger. However, the idea that only one specific part of the brain, the limbic system, deals with these emotions has been contested by some neuroscientists (Heimer et al., 2007)

(Adapted from Wilson and Stevenson, 2003; Heimer et al., 2007.)

Box 11.6   How to correct disconnected paragraph structure

Can you see how this corrects the structural problem of the disconnected mini-paragraph? Not only has it been absorbed into the larger paragraph, solving the immediate structural problem, but the main paragraph has been strengthened by gaining a sentence which provides a wider context, and later offers a potential link to a new paragraph, giving a sense of structural coherence.

Paragraphing methods

There are several models of paragraphs that you can use to help you express yourself effectively. The ones we'll present here are the ones that we think might be most useful to you in your written work. This isn't to suggest that you will, from now on, decide on which type of paragraph you want to use, and then write according to that exact model. However, if you are having difficulty getting started, or have a draft full of untidy paragraphs, then using these templates can, respectively, help you to either begin writing by building paragraphs block by block, or give you a sense of where your paragraphs have gone off course.

Building a paragraph by argument

This type of paragraph contains the following elements:

Topic sentence	What are you going to talk about in this paragraph? Clearly state this here. The reader should know exactly what to expect. The topic sentence should also link back to the main question in some way in order for the paragraph to be relevant.
Elaborating sentence	This should refine or elaborate on the general topic. What precise aspect of this topic are you going to talk about?
Data or evidence	Offer the reader data/evidence that you will discuss/ explain.
Explanation/discussion/ statement	Provide the explanation/discussion that the data requires.
Topic sentence 2/ conclusion/link	Conclude the paragraph. You should also remind the reader why the point you made is relevant to your essay/report question. You should have a sense of how the next paragraph relates to this one, and provide a link, or at least make the progression obvious.

Box 11.7 Detailed breakdown of paragraph structure

Here's a worked example, with each element clearly defined:

Topic Sentence – Students in the sciences have a variety of options open to them after they complete their undergraduate studies.

Elaborating Sentence – Many of these students choose to go on to study postgraduate degrees.

Data/Evidence – In 2015, approximately 5000 completed a leavers' survey. Of those students, 45% stated that they would be looking to apply for further study, with 34% opting to leave academia, and the remainder undecided.

Discussion – From this, we can see that postgraduate study is clearly the favoured option of the majority of students, much more so than going out into the wider workplace.

Topic Sentence 2/Conclusion/Link – But precisely which subjects do students go on to study at master's and PhD level?

Can you see how each sentence fits into the model to construct a coherent paragraph? You can also see what happens if you remove some of the components.

Many of these students choose to go on to study postgraduate degrees. In 2015, approximately 5000 completed a leavers' survey. Of those students, 45% stated that they would be looking to apply for further study, with 34% opting to leave academia, and the remainder undecided. From this, we can see that postgraduate study is clearly the favoured option of the majority of students, much more so than going out into the wider workplace. But precisely which subjects do students go on to study at master's and PhD level?

Box 11.8 Paragraph missing a topic sentence

When the paragraph lacks a topic sentence, then the reader does not always have the context required to fully understand the paragraph, or a sense of how it relates to the wider piece of work. Instead, the reader is thrown into the detail of the paragraph, without fully understanding why it is relevant. As you can see in this instance, omitting the topic sentence is particularly confusing, because it means that the rest of the paragraph talks generally about students, without the defining information in the topic sentence – science students.

Students in the sciences have a variety of options open to them after they complete their undergraduate studies. Many of these students choose to go on to study postgraduate degrees. From this, we can see that postgraduate study is clearly the favoured option of the majority of students, much more so than going out into the wider workplace. But precisely which subjects do students go on to study at master's and PhD level?

Box 11.9 Paragraph missing data/evidence

Now we don't have any evidence or data. Without this, we are forced to place complete trust in the writer's statement. On top of that, without the figures, we cannot analyse the data ourselves. The paragraph now appears weak and underdeveloped. A marker would have very good reason to single it out for criticism.

Students in the sciences have a variety of options open to them after they complete their undergraduate studies. Many of these students choose to go on to study postgraduate degrees. In 2015, approximately 5000 completed a leavers' survey. Of those students, 45% stated that they would be looking to apply for further study, with 34% opting to leave academia, and the remainder undecided. From this, we can see that postgraduate study is clearly the favoured option of the majority of students, much more so than going out into the wider workplace.

Box 11.10   Paragraph missing concluding/linking sentence

Now we have no link to the next paragraph. The paragraph stands on its own well enough, but without a link to the next paragraph, we lose a sense of how the essay might proceed. Also, without summarising the main point of the paragraphs, the sense of unity isn't quite so explicit.

Students in the sciences have a variety of options open to them after they complete their undergraduate studies. Many of these students choose to go on to study postgraduate degrees. In 2015, approximately 5000 completed a leavers' survey. Of those students, 45% stated that they would be looking to apply for further study, with 34% opting to leave academia, and the remainder undecided. But precisely which subjects do students go on to study at master's and PhD level?

Box 11.11   Paragraph missing interpretation of data

Without the sentence to summarise or interpret the evidence/data, the reader is left to draw conclusions on their own. That might not be too much of a problem in this paragraph, where the evidence offered is simple, and easy to interpret. However, in a paragraph where the data is complex and/or ambiguous, leaving your reader to draw their own conclusions without your input is risky, and might lead to misinterpretation. They may also think that you do not know how to analyse and discuss the material you've presented.

Building a paragraph by argument is a useful technique, and you can see, by removing individual parts, how robust the paragraph is when all parts are present.

Building a paragraph by detail

In this model, the paragraph is built through the accumulation of detail.

> The hippocampus is located in the medial temporal lobe of the brain, at the edge of the cerebral cortex (Watson et al., 2010). It can be further subdivided into the cornu ammonis and dentate gyrus. In turn, the dentate gyrus can be further broken down to the hilus and fascia dentata. It is often described as being shaped like a seahorse, hence the name – hippocampus – from the Greek hippos + kampos.
>
> (Adapted from Watson et al., 2010).

Box 11.12   Paragraph by detail

In terms of the general guidelines we discussed, the paragraph is unified through its description of one object. It is coherent in that it gradually builds a more detailed picture. It is fully developed in that it provides all the detail that the reader needs to know at this point.

Which details you choose to include, and which can be omitted, depend on what you are describing, and the depth you wish to go to in your description. This is an easy place to end up providing too much information, so keep things succinct. Make sure the description you provide is relevant to the overall purpose of your assignment.

Building a paragraph by process

Building a paragraph by process is a particularly valuable technique for science students, who often have to describe processes.

> **Essay question – Describe the key roles serotonin plays in the body**
>
> Serotonin (5-hydroxytriptamine) is a neurotransmitter. It plays a role in regulating the appetite (Bear et al., 2016). While dopamine is released in order to stimulate appetite, serotonin is released later, when food is being consumed. This activates the 5-HT2C receptor on cells that make dopamine, which has the consequence of preventing more dopamine from being released. This means that serotonin stops the appetite. This is only one role serotonin plays in the nervous system.
>
> (Adapted from Bear et al., 2016).

Box 11.13   Paragraph by process

There's a topic sentence that describes the unifying idea of the paragraph. There's also a concluding sentence which revisits the topic sentence and offers a possible link to the next paragraph (discussing another role that serotonin plays in the nervous system). The body of the paragraph is taken up with a description of the process by which serotonin inhibits appetite.

When writing a paragraph by process, think about the following:

- Consider whether the process is of an appropriate size to be the subject of one paragraph.
- Consider whether the process is too lengthy or detailed. If it is, then it might be too much for one paragraph to talk about in its entirety.
- Make sure you progress logically through the stages of the process, without leaving any gaps which might confuse your reader.

Building a paragraph by comparison and contrast

As you would expect, this is an especially useful paragraph model to use if you want to look at the relationship between two items, concepts, or processes, and draw out the similarities between them. Here's an example of what this kind of paragraph looks like in practice. This particular paragraph focuses more on drawing similarities:

> Enantiomers and diastereomers are both types of stereoisomers. They share the same molecular formula. They also share the same type of connectivity (Fox and Whitesell, 2004). However, while enantiomers are non-superimposable mirror images of each other, diastereomers are not. This means that while enantiomers share the same physical and chemical properties, diastereomers do not, and can have different physical and chemical properties. These different properties mean that diastereomers can be more readily purified than enantiomers.
>
> (Adapted from Fox and Whitesell, 2004).

Box 11.14   Paragraph by comparison and contrast

As you can see, it still follows the main guidelines for a paragraph. One central idea is discussed. That idea is fully developed through use of examples. The structure is coherent. The topic sentence lets the reader know the central idea of the paragraph. The concluding sentence refers back to the topic sentence, and offers a possible link to the next paragraph. The main structural feature of this type of paragraph is that the bulk of the paragraph consists of comparison.

Now that you have an idea of the structural models you can use to build paragraphs, let's look at how you can arrange your paragraphs to ensure a coherent flow throughout your writing

Structural techniques

Reverse outlining

Reverse outlining is a very useful editing technique which can be employed to help you keep track of your paragraphing, and decide whether it needs revision. The following steps should be followed:

1   Open a new document alongside the one you're working from.
2   Copy the first line of every paragraph, in order, and paste it into the new document.
3   Remember the first line of every paragraph should give the reader an indication of the main point that will be covered, and link the paragraph back to the main question.
4   As such, the list of first lines that you have created in this document should act as a bullet point overview of the whole essay/report/dissertation chapter.

Troubleshooting structural problems in the reverse outline

Look at the bullet point overview that you have created. How does it read?

- Look at the order of the bullet points. Is it coherent? Or is it jumbled? Can you rearrange them to create a better flow? It's easier to do that in this bullet point version of your work than it is in the full version, where reordering whole paragraphs can sometimes seem too extreme.
- Are there any obvious gaps? Is there an idea that you've forgotten to mention that would bridge this gap, and help your reader along? Check the bullet points on either side of the gap. Are either of them perhaps too broad, as was discussed before? Could one of the bullet points be splintered into two or three smaller points? Would that fill the gap?
- Alternatively, do you have bullet points which seem to be repeating themselves? It's easy, if you are very keen to demonstrate to your marker that you understand something, to repeat yourself across paragraphs, slightly tweaking the phrasing, but essentially saying the same thing each time. Look at the paragraphs in question and be ruthless when it comes to removing anything that's simply repetitive.

The main advantage of the reverse outline method is that it allows you to look carefully at the overall structure of your work without becoming distracted by the content, which is what can sometimes happen if you just read through the document as a whole. Here, you can see the skeleton of your discussion, and quickly and easily resolve any problems.

Reverse outlining can also act as an effective way to build a draft if you are having difficulty getting started. Writing a bullet point of every point you would like to cover, and then building a paragraph around that using one of the models offered here, is an effective way to start getting words on the page in a structured way.

Structure within paragraphs

Connectives

In our experience, students often express frustration and confusion when they receive feedback telling them that their work doesn't flow, or that there's no sense of progression. The idea of 'flow' seems vague, and difficult to articulate, and they don't understand how to begin to make their work do this.

As you saw above, there are paragraphing methods that can be used to ensure that there is a sense of progression in each paragraph, be that through argument, process, description or comparison/contrast. Considering what type of paragraph you have written, and the role it plays in the wider piece of writing, helps you avoid the 'information dump' paragraph, where the reader is presented with a block of information with no internal progression, and without its relevance to the question made explicit.

Another sure way of making sure that your writing exhibits logical progression and flow is to use connectives in your work. Connectives are another important way of adding clarity and coherence within paragraphs. Consider the following examples:

> The skills gained in the production of scientific writing stand students in good stead in the workplace. They can write concisely. They can write descriptively. They are of use to a number of different professions. Some of these professions may be unrelated to the sciences and offer opportunities the student had never considered. Scientific writing is a valuable skill to attain. It improves grades and it improves employment prospects.

Box 11.15   Paragraph without connectives

Crucially, the skills gained in the production of scientific writing stand students in good stead in the workplace. They can write concisely. They can **also** write descriptively. **Consequently**, they are of use to a number of different professions. Some of these professions may be completely unrelated to the sciences. **As such**, they may offer opportunities the student had never considered. **To summarise**, scientific writing is a valuable transferable skill to attain, **simultaneously** improving grades and employment prospects.

Box 11.16 Paragraph with connectives

Both paragraphs contain exactly the same information, presented in exactly the same order. Which do you find easier to understand? You can follow the progression of discussion in both, but the second example does the interpretative heavy lifting for the reader, guiding them carefully through the information, avoiding any scope for misunderstanding, and making it seem persuasive, as opposed to simply presenting them with a disconnected collection of facts.

As you can see from this example, connectives make clear exactly how pieces of information relate to each other. They take some of the burden of interpretation from your reader by making connections explicit, leading them through your discussion stage by stage. The overall result is a paragraph which flows much more easily, and which does not make excessive interpretative demands on your reader.

The table below gives examples of some commonly used connectives, and how they might be used in your writing. When you are reading over your drafts, look carefully at each paragraph. Circle all the connectives you find. If you can't find any, then ask yourself whether a connective might help your reader better follow your discussion.

Causal	Consequently, because, as a result, since, thusly
Temporal	Previously, next, while, when, simultaneously
Contrasting	However, alternatively, alternately, in contrast, in comparison, although, except, conversely, whereas
Additional	Also, additionally, first, second, third, moreover
Summarising	To conclude, to summarise, in brief, in short
Emphasis	Importantly, notably, indeed, crucially, particularly

Box 11.17 Common connectives and how they can be used

Conclusion

Structuring often presents students with difficulties, from dealing with the restrictions of working within a specific format, to crafting paragraphs and keeping sentence structure under control. The advice we have given you in this section enables you to take control of structure at every level of your writing and make it work for you, instead of letting it tie you up in knots. Using these techniques alongside the drafting methods we discussed at the beginning of the chapter will ensure that you convey your knowledge and ideas as clearly and coherently as possible, which will lead to higher grades.

Sounding Like a Scientist

Top 3 staff comments on tone:

► Colloquialisms sometimes creep in, causing tone problems.
► Erratic grasp of proper tone and voice is common.
► Word choice sometimes lacks accuracy.

Top 3 student comments on tone:

► I'm never sure exactly what I'm allowed to say – what's too informal, or too subjective.
► I know it's supposed to be in the passive voice, but I'm not really sure what that is, so I just try to copy the way I see other people write.
► Sometimes it just doesn't sound 'academic' enough.

When we use the word 'tone' in terms of writing, it describes the writer's attitude towards their topic and their reader. For example, you are likely to speak in an relaxed tone to your friends, but probably use a more business-like tone when you are speaking to a tutor. An unfavourable review of a film might have a hostile, cold, or dismissive tone, while a favourable review is likely to be respectful, or congratulatory in tone. Word choice, subjectivity and formality all play a role in the overall creation of tone.

Trying to master proper academic tone is something that students tell us they have difficulty with at various points in their academic career, whether they're writing their first essay, their dissertation, their PhD, or even journal articles.

This usually has to do with a lack of understanding of what tone is, and how it is created. It also often has to do with a sense of lacking confidence and ownership over your writing, which results in the idea that you have to write as someone else in order to sound convincingly academic. This is completely understandable in the early years of your degree, where you are still getting to grips with key concepts, and taking an authoritative tone can feel inappropriate.

The feeling of a lack of control over writing, that 'putting on' a writing voice stifles expression, as opposed to enabling it, can be heightened for science students, who sometimes already have anxieties about writing from school or college, and for whom the process might already seem alien and unpleasant.

Good academic writing expresses complex concepts clearly and coherently. It informs the reader, giving them exactly the information they need in order to follow the writer's reasoning, and then guides them carefully through that reasoning. Connections and patterns will be drawn out and fully explained. In concluding, the reader should understand why every piece of information was presented to them, and how it works together to answer the main question.

In terms of tone, academic scientific writing especially prizes the following qualities: **specificity, concision,** and **objectivity.**

Specificity in word choice

Although quibbling over exactly the right word to use might sometimes seem pedantic, specificity in word choice is important. Choosing the wrong word can blur your meaning or, at worst, completely alter it. We've found that students can sometimes lack precision in word choice, and often choose words that mean *roughly,* but not *exactly* what they want to convey. This can be damaging to an otherwise well-written piece of work, giving the impression of a lack of understanding, and making their observations and analyses seem less incisive than they actually are.

The following table contains the words that we've noticed students tend to confuse in their writing. It's by no means exhaustive, but should help you recognise these types of errors in your own writing, and also help you see why incorrect word choice can be so problematic. Remember, spell-check will not recognise any of these as errors, so it is important that you read with an eye for detail.

Easily confused words

Principal: The main part of something.	**Principle:** A moral or ideal.
Lose: To no longer possess something. To have less of something. To be unable to find something. To be defeated. To be unable to sustain something.	**Loose:** Not tight, or not firmly attached.
Can: To have the ability to do something.	**May:** To have permission to do something.
Affect: Generally speaking, this is the verb. To bring about a change or result.	**Effect:** Generally speaking, this is the noun. The result of a particular action or substance. 'The effect of adding the substance was obvious'.

Table 12.1   Easily confused words

Bisect: To divide something into two parts (usually equal parts).	**Dissect:** To cut something apart for the purposes of closer examination. From this comes the use of dissect to mean 'to analyse something in close, minute detail'.
Complement: Something which provides completion.	**Compliment:** To offer praise.
Advice: Advice is the noun. 'The following advice has been offered'.	**Advise:** Advise is the verb 'I would advise you to reject this proposal'.
Alter: Verb. To change something.	**Altar:** Noun. A table or platform.
Discreet: To be quiet and unobtrusive in order to avoid attention.	**Discrete:** Separate.
Farther: A greater distance. Refers to physical distance. 'The building is farther away than you might suspect'.	**Further:** Can mean more, or extra. 'This needs to be taken further' and can be placed before a noun. 'This requires further investigation'.
Beside: A preposition which refers to physical position. 'The instruments were placed beside the notebook'.	**Besides:** 'Apart from that' or 'aside from that'.

Table 12.1 *(Continued)*

Look out for these types of errors in your writing. A marker might be able to figure out which word you actually meant by looking at the context, but this is not always the case. Besides, an accumulation of errors like this gives a poor impression of your professionalism, and will make your marker wonder where else you might have been careless.

Concision and simplicity

It's easy to tie yourself in knots when choosing proper vocabulary to attain an appropriate tone. It's not uncommon, when trying to sound academic, for your word choice to wander instead into the overly formal and complicated. Remember, your writing needs to be context-appropriate, but also make your reader's life as easy as possible. Clarity and simplicity are best. Have a look at the following table:

Permitted the opportunity	Allowed
Utilise	Use
Commence	Begin

Table 12.2 Simple alternatives to complex words and phrases

Terminate	End
Fabricate	Make
Endeavour	Attempt
In the event that	If

Table 12.2   *(Continued)*

The words in the right column mean exactly the same as those in the left hand column, but they are clearer and shorter. Compare the following sentences:

> Utilising this instrument permitted the opportunity for the process to commence. In the event that a change was observed, the experiment would be terminated. (24 words)

> Using this instrument allowed the process to begin. If a change was observed, the experiment would be ended. (18 words)

The second sentence says exactly the same thing as the first, but is much clearer, and much less pompous. You'll also notice that it's much more concise. Six words might not seem like much of a difference in word count, but the cumulative effect across a whole essay will result in a much more succinct piece of writing.

The fact that these words are simpler does not mean that they are informal. Formality is not necessarily about complexity. It is about recognising the relationship between you and your reader, and using the vocabulary appropriate to that context.

Building a phrase book

When you're getting used to the vocabulary of a new type of writing, like scientific writing, it can be very useful to build a list of useful phrases you can use in your writing in order to introduce topics, describe trends, compare and contrast results – just as you would learn practical phrases if you were travelling to a foreign country.

This phrase-book will grow as you do more writing, and you will find that you favour some phrases more than others, moving towards developing your own style within the conventions of scientific writing. This type of book can also be of help when you find it difficult to phrase exactly what you want to say. For example:

> Substance A played a significant role in…
> Recent research indicates…
> This inconsistency could be attributed to…
> A practical approach to address this problem…

An extremely useful resource to help you build this list, especially for students with English as a second language, is the Manchester Academic Phrase Bank (www.phrasebank.machester.ac.uk). This is an online collection of generic academic phrases, grouped by function, which can be used without any fear of plagiarism. It is a good way of allowing you to become familiar with the appropriate level of language, as well as building your own repertoire of phrases. Similarly, *The Student Phrase Book* (Godfrey, 2013) provides useful definitions for common academic words and phrases, and allows you to see them in context in student writing.

General advice

- Avoid contractions: can't, won't, didn't, shan't, couldn't. These tend to be perceived as informal. Instead, always use the full version: cannot, did not, shall not, could not.
- Avoid colloquialisms and clichés. This isn't actually a very big problem in the majority of students that we see. When we do encounter it, it tends to be that an international student has used an informal phrase or word they hear it a lot in spoken English, and didn't realise that it was informal. Asking a friend on your course who has English as a first language to check for these kinds of errors can help. Take note of the phrases and words that are pointed out to you.
- Try to keep context in mind as you write. If you remember that you are working to gain a professional qualification, and that you are speaking to a professional in your chosen field, then issues such as using subject-specific terminology, communicating clearly, avoiding slang, and remaining objective all become self-evident.

Objectivity and the passive voice

One of the key differences between scientific writing and writing in the arts, or in the social sciences, is the use of the passive voice.

What is the passive voice?

The passive voice is a construction we use when the process is more important than the person performing it. For example, if you are writing a description of an experiment that you carried out, then it is very likely that you want your reader to focus on the process of the experiment itself, not the person carrying it out.

In order to do this we use a special construction called the passive voice. Look at the following:

> The **ethics committee** approved the **study.**

In this sentence, the ethics committee is the **subject** of the sentence. It is also **performing the action** in the sentence, 'approving the study'. The study undergoes the action, which makes it the **object** of the sentence. This is an active construction. In an active construction, we're most interested with the person performing the action.

Now, compare that sentence with this rewording.

> The **study** was approved by the **ethics committee.**

This is a passive construction. In a passive construction, we're not interested in the person performing the action. Instead, we're most interested in the thing **undergoing** the action.

This changes the emphasis in the sentence. In the first example, the ethics committee seemed fairly important. In the second example, the study, and the fact that it was approved, seems more important, because the writer has chosen to place it at the beginning of the sentence. The agent acting on the subject, the ethics committee, has been placed at the end of the sentence. In fact, if you decided that it was obvious that the ethics committee who approved the study, and that this information does not have to be included in the sentence at all, then it could be completely removed from the sentence.

> The study was approved.

If you think about this last example, then you can figure out one of the main reasons the passive voice is preferred in scientific writing. We use it when the person who carried out the process is not of interest or importance, and can therefore be removed from the sentence. Compare these sentences.

> I heated the mixture to approximately 24 degrees Celsius. When this temperature was reached, I checked for a precipitate. I established that the precipitate was present, and then I filtered this solution.

Box 12.1   Example of active voice

> The mixture was heated to approximately 24 degrees Celsius. When this temperature was reached, the flask was checked for the presence of a precipitate. On establishing this was present, the solution was filtered.

Box 12.2   Example of passive voice

It doesn't make much difference to the sentence when the person performing the action is removed, does it? They are unimportant here, where the focus instead is really on the process that is being carried out. As such, the passive voice is better for this type of writing.

Another reason scientific writing prefers the passive voice is to reinforce the impression of objectivity.

Generally speaking, students of virtually all university subjects are cautioned against subjectivity. The aim in academic writing is to offer objective observations and analysis based on a critical examination of facts and/or theory. When 'I' is used, there can be a tendency for personal opinion to creep into writing.

As you saw in the examples above, the passive voice can completely eliminate the actor from the sentence. There is no 'I'. The reasoning behind scientific writing's preference for this is that with 'I' completely removed, what is left can only be an impersonal observation and analysis of the facts.

In reality, it is worth noting that you could write an entire report in perfect passive voice and still be subjective in your interpretation of wider literature, or selective in how you reported your results. Increasing numbers of scientific journals specifically request that articles are written in the active voice, both to aid clarity and cut down on word count. However, as an undergraduate student, it is most likely that you will be requested to write in the passive voice.

Be careful in your use of the passive when the reader is likely to require more detail about who is performing the action. Consider the following example.

> It was suggested that this approach was flawed.

Who suggested this? Is this a commonly held opinion? Is this a point in the paragraph where you should be referring to a specific study? Would your reader want confirmation that you are aware of this study? You can still use the passive voice, but this is an example of where you might want to keep the agent in the sentence in the interests of clarity.

As mentioned previously, academic journals increasingly tend to prefer the active voice. As such, it can be interesting to note when the passive voice is used in any journal articles you read as part of your research. Why has the author chosen to omit the agent performing the action?

Writing in the past tense

Scientific writing uses the past tense to write about things that have already taken place: a process you carried out, or what someone else observed in the course of carrying out an experiment.

This one is worth mentioning because it can be tempting to write your methodology section like a recipe:

> Weigh 50 g of flour into a bowl. Add 2 eggs and 100 ml semi-skimmed milk. Mix thoroughly until the flour is wet through.

This is fine, but we wouldn't use a similar construction in science:

> Weigh 15 g sodium chloride, 7 g tryptone, and 7 g yeast extract. Add these powders to 500 ml distilled water and mix until thoroughly dispersed.

The distinction is that a recipe is known to work, and the chef who wrote it wants you to follow their instructions exactly so that you end up with a successful dish. In science, you carry out your methodology for your own purposes, and you write this down to explain how you arrived at the result you got. Your methodology is not guaranteed to be the best version possible, and there may be hundreds of different reasons that another researcher would want to vary your conditions. Methodologies are adapted every day in labs around the world. Perhaps someone doesn't have enough of a particular material and needs an alternative, or perhaps someone is running an experiment on a different scale. Instead of phrasing them like a recommendation, then, we just write them as a report, as you can see here:

15 g sodium chloride, 7 g tryptone, and 7 g yeast extract were added to 500 ml distilled water and mixed until thoroughly dispersed.

The present tense is for conclusions that you have drawn. The experiment which has already been carried out should be described in the past tense. The fact or concept it revealed should be discussed in the present tense.

The future tense is usually used for suggestions about how your work might be further developed, or put to different uses.

Conclusion

The aim of this chapter is not to give you a rigid set of rules which will restrict your range of expression while you write. By giving you an understanding of what tone means, how it is achieved, and helping you understand why certain conventions exist, you now know how to create the appropriate tone in your academic writing, and why it is important. Building up your own repertoire of commonly used words and phrases will help you feel comfortable and confident in expressing yourself. If you remember that scientific writing is a means of clearly communicating your thoughts to a specific audience, then you will write with clarity and coherence.

13

How to Say Exactly What You Mean

Top 3 staff comments on grammar:

► Sentences are often too long.
► The students have difficulty putting their point across.
► There's sometimes no understanding of basic punctuation.

Top 3 student comments on grammar:

► I'm not sure how to use a lot of it, and it stresses me out.
► It's probably not the most important aspect of scientific writing, so how much do I really need to focus on it?
► It was never explained at school, and now it seems really complicated.

When you're talking to someone, and you want to make sure you get your point across, you have a variety of different ways at your disposal to help you do this. You might try to speak especially slowly and clearly at key points. You might raise your voice for emphasis, or hold eye-contact, or use gestures. If, while you're talking, you happen to notice that the person you're talking to seems confused by one of your points, then you can rephrase it. If they really don't understand something, then they might ask you a question, which would allow you to clarify your point.

In writing, punctuation carries out all of these tasks. You can use punctuation to emphasise your points, to guide your reader through complex information, and to make sure that you communicate your understanding clearly and logically.

This chapter will make sure that you feel completely confident using punctuation to achieve this goal. Punctuation will be discussed in practical terms, in order to let you see exactly how and when to use it. After this, we will then move on to basic sentence structure. Again, practicality is key, discussing the advantages and disadvantages of each type of sentence, and when you might want to use each kind in your writing to help you express yourself.

After we've discussed everything you need to know, we will look at the most common student errors in punctuation, how to fix these, and prevent them from happening them in the first place. As we said, punctuation in writing works in the same way that your voice and facial expression, and gestures work in speech. If, mid-conversation, you were to suddenly lower your voice, or break eye contact and look in another direction, or take pauses in odd places, then your listener would find it difficult to follow what you were saying, and might even misunderstand you completely. Erratic punctuation has the same effect.

Punctuation

A clear understanding of the essential rules of punctuation will help you to express yourself more effectively, and feel more confident in your ability as a writer.

This section will not go into minute detail on every single fine point of punctuation, with lots of theoretical knowledge that you do not need to know. Instead, it will simply give you the tools you need to clearly and concisely convey your ideas to your reader.

The comma

The first piece of punctuation to look at in more detail is the comma. The comma is probably the most widely used and most versatile piece of punctuation. It can do a number of different jobs, which makes it very useful. However, this flexibility also means that it is easy to use it incorrectly, which can then cause confusion for your reader.

This section will outline the six main uses of the comma. It will then look at the most common errors that we see students make, and how these errors can be quickly and easily corrected.

Commas separate introductory elements (or connectives) from the rest of the sentence

Look at the following:

Firstly, appropriate materials were located and obtained.

However, this method did not prove helpful.

Consequently, it was decided that this approach could not be recommended.

In contrast, no reaction was observed in the second solution, despite our initial predictions.

You can see the connectives are all in bold at the beginning of each sentence. They might seem like small, unimportant words – but, as we discussed, they actually do an incredibly important job: telling your reader *exactly* how to interpret the information that follows. This aids clarity and flow, eliminates ambiguity, and ensures that your writing has a logical progression.

Think of connectives as a signpost. They *introduce* the content, but they're not *part* of the content. As such, connectives at the beginning of sentences (introductory elements) should be separated from the rest of the sentence with a comma.

Commas punctuate clauses in a compound sentence

A compound sentence contains two independent clauses (a clause which can stand on its own). These sentences must have a comma and a coordinating conjunction to link their two independent clauses. (This sentence type will be discussed in more detail later in the chapter.)

- The equipment was set up, and progress was carefully recorded.
- We spoke to several study participants, and we asked our list of pre-agreed questions.
- Tantalum metal is covered by a thin layer of oxide, so it does not react with air or water.

Commas separate dependent/subordinate clauses from the rest of the sentence

Dependent/subordinate clauses are parts of the sentence which contain additional information which is of less importance than the main point of the sentence. They give **extra** detail, or **clarify** the key point of the sentence in some way. However, they are not essential to our understanding of the sentence.

If you are having difficulties trying to identify subordinate clauses in your writing, then a good way of testing whether or not a clause is main or subordinate is to remove it from the sentence. If the sentence that remains still makes sense, <u>and</u> still makes the point you intended it to make, then what you removed is a subordinate clause. Don't worry if this doesn't seem clear just now – these sentences will be discussed in detail later on p.175. For now, just remember this use.

- Iridium, first discovered in 1803, is the most corrosion-resistant element known.
- Iridium is the most corrosion-resistant element known.

Source: WebElements [http://www.webelements.com/]

Equally, subordinate clauses tend to be easily mobile. You can put them in a different location within the sentence, and the sentence still makes sense.

- Iridium, first discovered in 1803, is the most corrosion-resistant element known.
- First discovered in 1803, Iridium is the most corrosion-resistant element known.

Source: WebElements [http://www.webelements.com/]

No matter where it goes, though, there must be either one or two commas (depending on the position of the clause) to inform that reader that it is secondary information.

Commas go around appositives

An appositive is a noun which names another noun. The idea is easiest to understand by looking at some examples. The first name for the noun is underlined, and the second name for the noun (the appositive) is in bold.

- The most abundant lanthanide, **Cerium**, is the principal component of mischmetal alloy.

Source: WebElements [http://www.webelements.com/]

- Infectious diseases that cause degeneration of the central nervous system, **transmissible spongiform encephalopathies**, can be found in humans and animals.

Source: WHO [http://www.who.int/bloodproducts/tse/en/]

Commas separate items in a list

You might already be familiar with this rule. You can choose to put a comma beside the final 'and' in the list. This is known as an Oxford comma. It can sometimes be useful for the sake of clarity, in case there is a risk that the final two items in the list might be seen as a compound item.

- The cerebral cortex is made up of four sections: the frontal lobe, the parietal lobe, the occipital lobe, and the temporal lobe.
- The major reaction components were sodium nitrates and phosphates, aluminium, and iron oxides.

Commas separate coordinate adjectives

If English is your first language, then you might not be aware that there is a very particular order in which adjectives are used. It goes as follows:

General opinion – specific opinion – size – shape – age – colour – nationality – material.

You can see this order within a sentence in these examples:

- We selected a **conical** (shape) **Perspex** (material) container.
- The study focused on **older** (age) **American** (nationality) males.

When the adjectives each come from a different adjective category, as they do in the examples given above, then they do not require a comma to separate them.

However, when the adjectives come from the same category, then a comma is required. For example,

The samples were stored in a cold (specific opinion), dark (specific opinion) room.

The comma – quiz

Questions
Try using commas to correct the following sentences and solidify your understanding of this concept before moving on to the rest of the chapter:
1. In order to ensure consistency the same method of recording results was employed in each experiment.
2. It is suggested that this approach should not be employed as this is an expensive time-consuming technique.
3. The results obtained showed an increase but this did not change our initial hypothesis.
4. Lithium, an alkali metal is highly reactive.
5. The diatomic elements are fluorine chlorine oxygen hydrogen nitrogen bromine and iodine.

Table 13.1 Comma quiz

Semicolons

Students often avoid using semicolons in their writing. However, semicolons can be very useful, and only have three easy rules surrounding their use.

Semicolons join two main clauses linked by sense

The first task they can perform is joining two main clauses that are linked by sense. You saw earlier that commas can also do this when aided by a coordinating conjunction (for, and, nor, but, or, yet, so). The semicolon provides a slightly stronger emphasis, making it especially useful when you want to draw attention to contrasting pieces of information. They can also help to indicate a sense of progression from one idea to the next. This can help you emphasise development in your writing, while still keeping everything concise.

- The samples in the first tray exhibited a change; the samples in the second tray remained the same.
- The participants in the first study reported overall weight gain; the participants in the second study reported a loss.

The clauses on either side of the semicolon could stand as a complete sentence on their own. You could, if you chose, write them as two separate sentences. However, if the sentences are connected by sense, and offer an important comparison of some sort, then combining them by using a semicolon helps to draw your reader's attention to this.

Semi-colons punctuate two main clauses linked by a transitional phrase or a conjunctive adverb

This use is similar to the one just discussed, except that there will also be a transitional phrase or conjunctive adverb in the middle of the two clauses.

A conjunctive adverb works like the coordinating conjunctions we looked at in the section on commas. They connect two complete ideas, and also help you to understand how those ideas are related. The table below gives an example of some common conjunctive adverbs.

Thus	However	Moreover	Consequently
Also	Besides	Still	Therefore
Otherwise	Hence	Finally	Indeed
Then	Meanwhile	Likewise	Accordingly
Next	Instead	Similarly	Still
Nevertheless	Conversely	Furthermore	Equally

Table 13.2   Common conjunctive adverbs

The solution in the first beaker remained colourless; **conversely**, the solution in the second beaker demonstrated a colour change.

Plant cells contain high levels of potassium, which is obtained from soil; **consequently**, farmland requires potassium fertiliser in order to maintain adequate levels for crop growth.

The study explained that the equipment required for this process had been unobtainable; **similarly**, the materials required had been too expensive to obtain.

These conjunctions sometimes appear **within** clauses, in which case they only need to be punctuated with commas. When they connect two main clauses, as they do in the examples above, then they require a semicolon. They then require a comma afterwards, because they act like an introductory element for the second main clause.

Separating phrases in a list

The next task that semicolons can perform is to separate long phrases in a list.

The results allowed three main conclusions to be drawn: that substance A had a lowering effect on blood pressure; that substance B had no effect at all; and that neither substance was well-tolerated by the test subject.

This can also be very helpful in avoiding confusion when some of the phrases in the list contain commas.

There were three ways that the experiment might have been performed: the first was efficient, but expensive; the second was time-consuming and dangerous; and the third was expensive, lengthy, and difficult.

Can you see how the semicolons aid clarity in the previous example, and help to keep the phrases within the list clearly separated?

The semicolon – quiz

Questions
Try using semicolons, and commas, where appropriate, to correct the following sentences and solidify your understanding of this concept before moving on to the rest of the chapter
1. Many studies omitted this detail in fact, it is vital.
2. There were four important decisions made: the first seemed vital but it did not impact results.
3. The results obtained showed an increase but this did not change our initial hypothesis.
4. Lithium, an alkali metal is highly reactive.
5. The diatomic elements are fluorine chlorine oxygen hydrogen nitrogen bromine and iodine.
6. The results confirmed our initial thought moreover they confirmed the hypotheses of several other studies.

Table 13.3   Semicolon quiz

Colons

Like semicolons, we've found that students tend to avoid using colons in their writing, because they're not very sure of how to use them properly. However, the colon is actually a very simple piece of punctuation. It only has two jobs, both of which can be very useful in your writing.

Colons introduce a formal list

First of all, the colon can be used to introduce a formal list, that is, a list which is important or particularly long. This might be particularly useful if you are providing the reader with a list of equipment or materials used in an experiment, or a list of parameters used to select participants, and you want to make sure that they know this list is important.

- Participants were selected on the basis of the following criteria: age, sex, activity level, and body mass index.
- The following equipment was used: a burette, a burette stand, a clamp, a beaker, and a pipette.

Can you see how the colon has been used in both examples? The reader is forced to pause, and then pay particular attention to the list that follows. This makes it a useful piece of punctuation to use when you want to draw the reader's attention to something.

Announcing an explanation or amplification

The colon only has one other task that it can perform: indicating that an explanation or an amplification is about to follow. Can you see how it did that in the previous sentence?

- There was one common factor in all of the findings: raised levels of chloride ions.
- Every previous researcher identified the same key difficulty: cost.

Can you see how the job the colon does here is very similar to the job it does before a list? Again, it forces the reader to pause before continuing with the sentence. The reader has to reflect on the part of the sentence they have just read, and then pay attention to the information that follows.

You are unlikely to use colons too often in one piece of writing. They are fairly dramatic pieces of punctuation, and best used to draw your reader's attention to important pieces of information, as you have seen. When you are writing your product draft, look out for places that they could be usefully employed to grab your reader's attention and ensure that you get your point across.

The colon – quiz

Questions
Try using colons to punctuate the following sentences and solidify your understanding of this concept before moving on to the rest of the chapter.
1. One key detail was omitted, time.
2. There were four important decisions made; the first seemed vital, but it did not impact results.
3. The results obtained showed a change in the following, temperature, mass, and reactivity.
4. The diatomic elements are fluorine chlorine oxygen hydrogen nitrogen bromine and iodine.

Table 13.4 Colon quiz

Most common mistakes in student writing

Now that you have a practical grasp of all the punctuation you need, you can use it with confidence to ensure that you communicate clearly with your reader. You are probably unlikely to find yourself instantly using every single piece of punctuation flawlessly in your process drafts. This is fine, and nothing to worry about. As was discussed previously, the process draft is simply the place to get words on the page as a way of working through your own understanding and ideas.

Instead, when you are writing your product draft, you can look carefully at how to communicate your content as clearly as possible by using appropriate punctuation. Which points need to be broken down in order to be clearly explained? Which comparisons require emphasis? Are there any lists that you want to make sure your reader pays attention to?

Equally, you should try to keep a careful eye out for any punctuation errors you know you tend to make. Look back at the questions after each section. Were there any that you found difficult? Look out for these pieces of punctuation in your product draft, and check that you've used them correctly.

These are the most common errors that we find in student writing. Check your work to see if you can find any of them.

Comma splicing

In the section on the comma, we saw that it is a very versatile piece of punctuation, able to perform six tasks in your writing. While it is versatile, it is also weak. This means that one job it cannot do alone in your writing is linking two main clauses.

> The samples in the first tray exhibited a change, the samples in the second tray remained the same.

The clauses on either side of the comma could stand on their own as complete sentences, which makes them main clauses. Commas are too weak to join two main clauses.

So how can we correct this? We have three options:

1. Use a semicolon instead
The samples in the first tray exhibited a change; the samples in the second tray remained the same.

Table 13.5   Ways to correct comma splices

2. Make them two separate sentences
The samples in the first tray exhibited a change. The samples in the second tray remained the same.
3. Use a comma and a coordinating conjunction
The samples in the first tray exhibited a change, but the samples in the second tray remained the same.

Table 13.5   *(Continued)*

Run-on sentences

A run-on sentence is similar to a comma splice, in that two main clauses have been joined inappropriately. While the comma splice incorrectly uses a comma to do this, the run-on sentence uses nothing at all.

> The next part of the process was time-consuming work was started on it immediately

Here, we have two main clauses jammed together with no attempt to use punctuation to link them. This is corrected in exactly the same way as the comma splice sentence:

1. Use a semicolon
The next part of the process was time-consuming; work was started on it immediately.
2. Make them two separate sentences
The next part of the process was time-consuming. Work was started on it immediately.
3. Use a comma and a coordinating conjunction
The next part of the process was time-consuming, so work was started on it immediately.

Table 13.6   How to correct a run-on sentence

The overall effect of the comma splice and run-on sentence error is to fatigue and confuse your reader. This is because too many important facts and ideas are run together, with no time to fully absorb what they mean, and no guidance on how to interpret them.

Misused semicolons

Semicolons either tend to be completely absent, or used in place of commas. Remember the basic rules:

- Are you connecting two main clauses? A semicolon can be used here.
- Are you writing a long and complex list? Semicolons might help you keep things clear.

Colons

Colons tend to be entirely absent. You now know how they can be used.

- Have you made a statement which you now want to explain? A colon can be used here.
- Are you introducing an important list? A colon can be used here.

Sentence types

There are four basic sentence ways that sentences can be structured. Understanding how each is constructed will improve the style of your writing by showing you the most effective way to present different types of information. It will also help you to avoid structural problems, and proofread more effectively.

Before sentence types are discussed in detail, you need to understand **clauses**.

A clause is a group of words which express a thought. Some clauses can stand on their own, while others need a main clause in order to make sense.

Look at the previous sentence:

> **Some clauses can stand on their own**, while others need a main clause in order to make sense.

The bold section of the sentence could stand alone as a complete sentence. We don't need any more information for it to make sense. However, the other half of the sentence cannot stand alone. We would not know what 'others' referred to without the information at the beginning of the sentence. It requires the first half of the sentence to provide context. Try reading it aloud if you are unsure.

Clauses that can stand on their own are known as independent clauses. Clauses which require help in order to make sense are known as dependent clauses.

- **Simple** sentences contain one independent clause.
- A **compound** sentence contains two independent clauses.
- A **complex** sentence has one independent clause and at least one dependent clause.
- A **complex/compound** sentence has two independent clauses and one dependent clause.

- I read books. (**Simple**)
- I read books and I write reviews. (**Compound**)
- I read books, which are usually fiction. (**Complex**)
- I read books and I write reviews, which are occasionally published. (**Complex/ Compound**)

Simple sentences

Simple sentences are particularly useful in our writing when we want to express one idea or thought very strongly, and make sure our reader pays attention to it.

- Our results were inconclusive.
- The implications of the experiment are clear.
- This result has great significance for the wider field.

Compound sentences

A compound sentence consists of at least two independent clauses. It can be punctuated in the following ways:

A coordinating conjunction and a comma

A conjunction is a linking word. A coordinating conjunction means that the information before and after the conjunction is of equal importance. The coordinating conjunctions are as follows:

For, and, nor, but, or, yet, so

These conjunctions help us understand the relationship between pieces of information.

- The study was well-funded, but we still ran out of money.

- Several attempts were made to ensure consistency, yet the results still indicated problems.

A semicolon

Semicolons can be used to link the independent clauses in a compound sentence. This is particularly useful if you want to present two contrasting but linked pieces of information, and draw your reader's attention to this comparison.

- Some students enjoy group work; others find it draining.
- The investigator assumed this approach would be successful; this was not the case.

Complex sentences

Complex sentences contain one independent clause, and at least one dependent clause. This means that there will be one main piece of information, and then a piece of information that relies on the other half of the sentence to provide meaning. The independent clause is in bold, the dependent clause is not.

- After she'd written the first draft, **she emailed her tutor.**
- **The solution was carefully observed,** in order to ensure accurate results.

Note that the independent clause can occur in the first or second half of the sentence.

If you're having difficulty deciding which part of the sentence is the dependent/subordinate clause, then try to look out for subordinating conjunctions.

Look at the two example sentences above. The dependent/subordinate clause is introduced by the following words/phrases:

> In order
> After

As discussed earlier in the chapter, compound sentences use coordinating conjunctions, which indicate that the information on either side of the sentence is of equal importance. Subordinating conjunctions, on the other hand, indicate that the information that follows is of less (subordinate) importance.

The following table contains a list of the most common subordinating conjunctions and the relationship they suggest between the pieces of information in the sentence:

Relationship	Subordinating Conjunction
Cause/Effect	because, since, so that
Comparison/Contrast	although, even though, though, whereas, while
Place and Manner	how, however, where, wherever
Possibility/Conditions	if, whether, unless
Relation	which, who
Time	after, as, before, since, when, whenever, while, until

Table 13.7 Subordinating conjunctions

Compound-complex sentences

Compound-complex sentences contain two independent clauses and one dependent clause. Look at the example below.

> **We decided that the article was too complicated, but our students**, who like challenging themselves, **thought that we were wrong**

Compound-complex sentences are long, and are usually trying to convey complex information. It's important to be clear on which information is of primary importance, and which is of secondary importance, and then punctuate appropriately. If you're unsure, then the sentence can usually be broken down to make it easier to handle, like this:

> **We decided that the article was too complicated. However, our students**, who like challenging themselves, **thought that we were wrong.**

That's not to say that compound-complex sentences should be avoided. They can be a very effective way of expressing detailed information. However, if you are going to use them, ask yourself whether

A. All the information contained in the sentence needs to be there and
B. If the information might be easier to understand in a simpler sentence structure.

When you're editing:

Look for long sentences

1 Do they have a main point? If not, think about creating two or more short sentences.
2 If it does have a main point, then make sure that any subordinate clauses are clearly demarcated with commas.
3 Could the information be presented more effectively using parallel structures?
4 Are there compound/complex sentences? Look for main clauses. Have you punctuated these properly?

Look for compound sentences

1 Has the sentence been punctuated correctly? If it has, look more carefully. Might it actually be more effective and easier to understand as two separate sentences?
2 If you are drawing attention to the contrast between two pieces of information, would a semicolon help underline this comparison?

Look for simple sentences

1 Is this a complete sentence? Make sure that it's not a fragment masquerading as a sentence.

In practice

As we said when we looked at punctuation, do not worry about trying to implement all of this immediately in your writing. Write your process drafts as normal, without worrying about structure. Then, when you come to your product draft, think about exactly what information you want to convey in each paragraph. Do you want to draw your reader's attention to a comparison? Use a compound sentence. Do you want to state a single fact clearly, or make an important statement? Use a simple sentence. If you have a detailed piece of information you want the reader to understand, then use a complex or compound-complex structure to carefully express your main points and supporting detail.

No matter which sentence type you choose to employ, it important to think about how your reader will interpret the information offered within each structure.

For example, if you accidentally put important information inside a subordinate clause, then you are signalling that it is of less importance than the rest of the sentence, to the extent that it could safely be removed without losing the main meaning of the sentence. This is likely to cause confusion, and the reader might completely misinterpret your meaning.

If you have a very important fact or finding that you want to make sure your reader pays close attention to, then burying it in a very long sentence is a bad idea, because it will get lost amongst other information.

Let's look at an example paragraph to see how this all works in practice.

Describe the role played by neurons in the central nervous system

Neurons are the main component of the central nervous system (Bear et al., 2016). They are each made up of a soma, an axon, and dendrites. There are specialised types of neurons that do specific jobs: sensory neurons, interneurons, and motor neurons. They can also be subdivided by morphology: bipolar, multi-polar, and pseudo-unipolar. Neurons send and process information via chemical and electrical signalling. This is known as neurotransmission, which is enabled by ion channels which allow charged ions to flow across the cell membrane.

(Adapted from Bear et al., 2016).

Box 13.1   Paragraph with varying sentence structures

Let's look at the first two sentences.

Neurons are the main component of the central nervous system. They are each made up of a soma, an axon, and dendrites.

We have two simple sentences here, each of which states a fact. You could choose to structure it differently.

Neurons, which are each made up of a soma, an axon, and dendrites, are the main component of the central nervous system.

Now we've made it a complex sentence. The information about neuron structure has been turned into a subordinate clause, and nested in the middle of the sentence. Do you think this changes how you to interpret the sentence? Does the information about structure carry quite the same importance? Is it easier, or more difficult, to take in the information now that it's all contained in one sentence?

What about the end of the paragraph?

> Neurons send and process information via chemical and electrical signalling. This is known as neurotransmission, which is enabled by ion channels which allow charged ions to flow across the cell membrane.

Do you think that 'this is known as neurotransmission' would be stronger as a simple sentence? Or do you feel that it is important to attach a subordinate clause explaining how it takes place? Would you prefer to completely restructure it?

> Neurons send and process information via chemical and electrical signalling. This process is enabled by ion channels, which allow charged ions to flow across the cell. This sending and processing is known as neurotransmission.

There is no right or wrong answer in any of these alternatives. The aim is to demonstrate how much more control you, the writer, have over your work when you have a grasp of sentence structure. This means, in turn, that you can fully demonstrate your understanding of your work in your written assignments.

Conclusion

An understanding of punctuation and sentence structure gives you control over your writing, and allows you to communicate clearly and precisely. You now understand how to trim long sentences in order to assist your reader's understanding of your work, and when shorter sentences are more appropriate to make strong, impactful point. Now that you're familiar with different types of sentence, you know which to use to ensure that you fully and clearly convey your points. You now have a practical understanding of the punctuation you need in order to write effectively. Instead of giving you an exhaustive overview of every little detail of grammar, we've given you just what you need to write effectively. You are now in charge of the grammar, instead of the other way round. This is of value in any kind of writing, and will definitely be useful in the long term.

Editing and Proofreading Your Work

Top 3 staff comments on editing and proofreading:

► We always tell students they should produce multiple drafts, but their assignments often suggest that they haven't done this.
► The lack of drafting is possibly due to poor time-management. Students don't recognise the importance of drafting.
► It's frustrating when you read an assignment that could have been substantially improved with some time spent on editing. Lots of small errors make work look careless.

Top 3 student comments on editing and proofreading:

► I'm never exactly sure what I'm doing right or wrong, so how can I check for things that need to be fixed?
► I just don't have time.
► If I leave it until too close to the deadline, the idea of reading through and finding mistakes just makes me more nervous.

While students often see 'checking their work' as one task, editing and proofreading are actually two very different activities. You will find that you will work more quickly, more effectively, and produce cleaner final drafts if you keep them separate.

Let's look at each in more detail, and how they can benefit your work.

What is editing?

Editing involves looking at several different aspects of the assignment. It doesn't look at the fine detail in terms of wording and punctuation, but instead examines the work on a deeper level. It deals with how the content has been conveyed via your structure. Editing might reveal that the work could be better organised in order to effectively present your ideas.

Before you begin to edit, we recommend taking a couple of days away from your draft. It can be difficult to be objective and look at it as a whole when you've been focused on details. After you've taken a break, you can come back to it with fresh eyes and look at the following.

Check content

First of all, no matter which type of assignment you've been set: have you actually done what was asked of you? Check the question again. Make sure you have fully responded to the command in the question, and not just written generally on the topic. The content needs to be entirely relevant to the question/task set. If you are at all unsure on how to do this, then look back again at the chapter on deconstructing the question.

It's surprisingly easy to include material that is tangentially related to the question set, but that is not actually directly relevant. It's also surprisingly difficult to make yourself remove material like this. In early assignments, it's natural to feel anxious about wanting to do well. Students often deal with this by trying to include absolutely everything they know in their assignment, whether it's relevant or not. This will not help you get better grades. In fact, given that markers often have 'relevance' and 'structure' as part of their marking criteria, it's actually more likely to hurt your chances of doing well.

If you find it difficult to delete material like this after taking the time to write it, open a new word document while you're editing. When you remove material from the main draft, paste it into this document, and save the document as something like 'supplementary information'. It will be useful later for exam revision, or a later assignment. Whatever you use it for, putting it in a new document, instead of just deleting it, will make it easier to remove from your draft.

Editing your report

If you are writing a report, does each section contain the appropriate content? You can go back and look at Chapter 2 for a detailed breakdown if you are still unsure what should go in each section, or use the following as a checklist for editing purposes.

Abstract

The abstract should act as a concise summary of the whole report. It does a crucial job in allowing the reader to get an overview of your work and decide whether they want to read the entire report.

It should do the following:

- Clearly state your objective.
- Briefly describe the methods used.
- Succinctly describe the most important results.
- Summarise the conclusions that can be drawn from those results.

Possible issues

Don't be tempted to start giving details of results in the abstract. This is the place for a summary of key results, not an exhaustive list of all of them.

Introductions

The introduction should clearly state your research question, justify why the question is worth answering, and set your work in context. It should do the following:

- State the research question.
- Explain why the research question is worth examining.
- Briefly summarise relevant literature in order to provide context.
- Clearly and concisely define any key concepts and/or terms.

Possible issues

Make sure you draw a link between wider literature and your work. The literature is there to provide context for your report, not simply as proof that you have read what's on the reading list.

Methods

This section of the report should describe your methods and materials clearly and in enough detail that someone else could repeat your experiment. It should:

- be written in the past tense, since these are actions you have already carried out;
- be written in the passive voice, since you are focusing on the process;
- contain an explanation of why you chose this particular method;
- contain an explanation of why you used these specific materials;
- be structured in a way that makes it as easy as possible for the reader to find the information they need.

Possible issues

Materials and methods can be included as two headings within this section to avoid confusion if necessary.

Be careful not to wander into talking about results at this point.

Results

This section of the report should clearly describe your results. It should be as unambiguously written as possible. *Explanations* of the results should not take place here. The results sections should:

- describe your results;
- highlight any particularly important results;
- ensure that any graphs and tables are clearly labelled.

Possible issues

This is not the place to interpret results. Make sure this section is only descriptive, and save interpretation for the discussion section.

Graphs and tables that are poorly labelled, or not labelled at all, only confuse your reader.

Discussion

The discussion section of the report should clearly and coherently explain your results, and talk about the wider significance of your findings. It should:

- interpret your results;
- link your findings to other literature in the field;
- assess whether the questions raised in the introduction have been answered;
- critically analyse any limitations you think the work had (problems with experimental design);
- be written in the past tense when describing actions you carried out in the past;
- be written in the present tense when discussing the implications of your work.

Possible issues

Make sure you relate your interpretation of your results back to the introduction.

Don't just discuss literature that agrees with your findings. Be prepared to explain any differences or contradictions.

Draw out any patterns in your results and explain these. Equally, don't conceal any unexpected results.

Are there wider practical or theoretical implications? Discuss these.

Editing your essay

Introductions

The introduction plays a crucial role in the essay. We've found that students can often become worried about how to start essays, which leads them to leave the introduction until last. However, the introduction actually has a very specific set of tasks to perform, which makes it easy to write.

If you are writing an essay, then you should make sure that your introduction:

- deconstructs the essay question;
- clearly defines any important terms;
- clearly states the essay's purpose/argument;
- tells the reader in detail the main points the essay will make;
- gives an indication of the essay's conclusion.

When you are writing your introduction, you should cover each of the bullet points listed in the box above. After you have done this, you will have produced a paragraph which acts as a set of guidelines for you as the writer, and for your reader. You can refer back to it as you write to remind yourself of the purpose of the essay, the points that you promised you would cover (which should each correspond to one paragraph), and the conclusion you should be working towards.

This is not to say you should be inflexible. If, as you are writing, you realise there is an extra point you want to cover, or you want to modify your conclusions, then you can go back to the introduction to reflect this. Make sure, though, that you are not deviating from the essay question, or including irrelevant material.

When the introduction is finished, it should act like a signpost for your reader, clearly describing your essay's destination, and the steps it will go through to get there. A good introduction lets your marker know that you have understood the question, and allows them to anticipate how your essay is going to proceed.

A rushed or jumbled introduction, on the other hand, makes your reader's life more difficult. Instead of giving them the information they need at the outset of your essay, you are asking them to search for all this as they read the body of your work. Likewise, your life is made more difficult, because, without a clear introduction, it is very easy to wander from the essay question, and for there to be gaps and repetitions in the body of the work.

We've found that problems with introductions tend to arise when you've not fully carried out the note-taking and planning stage, but have started to write the essay anyway. This often leads to an overly general introduction which doesn't really say anything at all, or an introduction which doesn't match up with the content of the essay, both of which are very confusing for your reader, and for you.

It's easy to want to do this when you are anxious about a deadline and just want to start writing. However, you are only really making the whole process more time consuming and stressful. If you are not fully informed on the topic, and confident about what you want to say, then you run the risk of producing an essay which omits key pieces of information, and which sounds uncertain and unfocused, both of which are issues which will cause your grade to drop.

You'll also spend the writing time constantly heading back to your reading list to fill in the gaps in your knowledge. This can lead you to doubt your abilities, and this lack of confidence will be reflected in your writing. It will also make the writing experience itself unpleasant and stressful, which is something we'd like to avoid.

Overall

Take the time to produce a clear and thorough introduction. Don't worry about making it stylish. Aim for clarity. Follow the steps listed above, and write clearly and thoroughly. The finished introduction should account for around 10% of the overall length of the essay.

Essay body

The body of the essay contains the majority of the content, and is where you will pick up most of your marks. There are a number of different points you should check.

Each paragraph should make one clear point. That point should be backed up, where appropriate, with data that demonstrates to the reader how you have arrived at this conclusion. You should check each paragraph to make sure that any statement you have made are adequately supported by evidence. Conversely, if you have tables/figures/data, then you should contextualise these by explaining to the reader what they mean, and how they are relevant to your discussion.

There should be a logical progression from one paragraph to the next. Sections and paragraphs can have headings if you feel that this makes your structure clearer and easier to follow.

The body of the essay should consist of paragraphs which are:

- fully relevant to the essay question;
- built on each other in a logical flow;
- linked;
- built around one main point.

We've found that problems with the body of the essay tend to arise when:

1 **You've not taken the time to plan before you start writing**
This will usually lead to a very confused first draft. As we discussed, it's fine for the process draft to be unstructured and require revision, but if you start to write with no idea at all of what you want to say, you're unlikely to produce much of value that can be edited later.

2 **Your internal paragraph structure could use extra work**
Paragraphs need to have one unifying idea, which is followed coherently throughout. This is aided by using the paragraph structure types we suggested in the previous chapter. If you are remotely unsure about how to build a paragraph, then it's easy to end up with paragraphs that lack focus, and wander from one point to another, disrupting the overall structure of your essay.

3 **You've not done all the research and thinking you need to do before writing**
This is likely to lead to paragraphs which contain statements or ideas without adequate evidence to back them up, or which are not contextualised in the wider scientific literature. As such, the paragraphs are likely to be rather short and weak. Alternatively, you might have paragraphs full of unexplained data. These might be overly long, but deficient in actual content in terms of your contribution, which is ultimately what your marker is looking for.

The body of the essay is likely to be successful when a sound understanding of the essay question is coupled with a grasp of paragraphing structure. Try to remember that each paragraph should only cover one main point, and that the reader should be led through your overall essay in a logical progression.

Conclusions

The conclusion should:

- clearly restate the question;
- summarise how each of your main points have been covered;
- not contain any new material.

Conclusions can sometimes cause students confusion. Much like introductions, though, they have a very specific job to do. Once you know what that is, you should find them easier to write.

Conclusions should restate the purpose stated in the introduction, and summarise the points you made in the body of the essay. You should then state your conclusion(s). Conclusions sometimes contain recommendations for future research, but this might not be appropriate in the early stages of your degree.

We've found that problems with conclusions tend to arise when:

1 **Your ideas have changed while you were writing, and now the essay is no longer coherent and unified**
   This whole issue can be neutralised if you follow the process/product model we suggested in Chapter 12. The process draft is the place to iron out this kind of issue. If you haven't followed this model, then you will need to go back and look carefully at your introduction, consider carefully how it needs to be rewritten to reflect your changed ideas, and adjust the structure of the body of the essay to make sure it fits your new approach.

2 **You start to rewrite the whole essay in the conclusion**
   The key here is to be concise. You are being asked to summarise the main points of the essay, not rewrite them in full using slightly different wording. It's easy to want to write it all again if you are anxious about convincing the reader you understand the subject but, as you did your job properly in the body of the essay, this won't be required.

Remember that your conclusion has two main tasks it needs to perform. If you can ensure it does these, then it will be a successful conclusion. Keep it concise. Like the introduction, it should account for around 10% of the overall length of the essay.

When you read over your essay as a whole, you should try to go through the following stages to ensure that you have produced a coherent piece of work, and to ensure that you spot and address any issues.

Look carefully at your introduction. Take note of the points you said you would cover. Now look at the paragraphs in the body of the essay. Does each paragraph contain one point, and does that one point match up to what you said you would cover in your introduction? If not, ask yourself:

- Is this paragraph relevant to the essay question? If not, remove.
- Is this a point that developed as I wrote, and now deserves to be added to the introduction?
- Should the listing of points in the introduction be made more specific?

Now look at the paragraphs in the body of the essay. You should be able to sum up each paragraph in one sentence. Write this in the margin. To make this step even more effective, look at this summary of the paragraph, and check whether the paragraph style suits the point. If, for example, the paragraph compares two materials, then a compare/contrast style paragraph would be best.

If you can't sum up the paragraph in one sentence, then take a closer look at it. Is the topic too big, meaning that you can't sum it up in one sentence? Look at how this can be broken down into two or more paragraphs. If it's not too big, but still can't be summed up in once sentence, then read the paragraph carefully. Has your point shifted or progressed at some point, so that the paragraph is no longer unified? Again, look at whether you should make a new paragraph.

After you have done this, you should have a collection of sentences summarising each paragraph.

- Do these points cover everything you set out to discuss in the introduction? Is there a point that you now notice is missing? If so, expand that missing point into a paragraph.
- Do any of the points repeat themselves? If so, read those respective paragraphs again. Have you repeated yourself, perhaps with slightly different phrasing? This is very easy to do, especially if you're anxious to make sure the reader has fully understood the point you're trying to make. Remove one of the repetitive paragraphs, and make sure the remaining paragraph is as clearly written as possible.
- Read the sentences through in order. Is there logic to how they are arranged? Does each build on the last? Make sure that there is some sort of flow, whether it comes from coherent discussion, or describing the stages in a process.

What is proofreading?

Editing, as you've seen, is about looking at the 'bigger' aspects of your work: ensuring that the content is appropriate to the question asked, that each section contains appropriate content, and that the overall piece of work is coherent and does the job asked of it.

Proofreading is primarily about spotting errors in punctuation and spelling. Although these types of errors might seem less important than understanding of content, or appropriate structuring, an accumulation of errors can make your work look careless. On top of that, certain errors can make your work difficult to understand, hindering you from fully conveying your understanding and ideas.

Proofreading requires a careful eye for detail. If you become bored or fatigued, then you will miss mistakes. Try the following steps to improve your proofreading skills:

Only proofread for one kind of error at a time

Proofreading demands a high level of concentration. It's best to make sure that concentration is not divided by trying to find every possible type of error at once. This is where paying attention to feedback from previous assessments can be of great benefit. If your markers have pointed out, for example, that you have a tendency to use semicolons incorrectly, and that there's certain words you persistently misspell – then look out for those particular errors.

If you know that you have problems with a particular piece of punctuation, then highlight or circle each instance of that punctuation mark, and check that you have used it correctly.

Try to avoid spending hours at a time proofreading

Proofread for 20 minutes maximum. It's a task that demands a lot of attention. If you set aside hours to proofread, then it's easy to lose concentration and miss mistakes, because you will become tired and bored.

Read your work aloud, exactly as punctuated

This is a gold standard for proofreading. Your ear will instantly pick up on errors that your eye will simply glide over on the page. We have used this technique with students from first-year to PhD level, and it always yields excellent results. You might also find that reading your work aloud will help you spot instances where paragraph or sentence order should be changed in order to make the work read more logically. In the longer-term, it will also give you a sense of how small punctuation errors can damage flow in your writing, which will help you avoid these problems in future.

This will not only result in a cleaner assignment, but will also benefit your writing style as a whole, as you will learn to pick up on awkward phrasings, or overly long sentences. If you find it difficult at first, then ask a friend if they are willing to read it aloud for you. Sometimes hearing your work in someone else's voice helps give you the distance you need in order to be critical of it.

Take some time away from the assignment

It can sometimes be difficult to get enough distance from an assignment to proofread it effectively. If you've been working on something for several weeks, then you can become too familiar with the document, and stop seeing errors.

On top of that, if you are anxious about getting a good grade, then it can be easy to get caught up in the content as you read.

If you've been proofreading from the screen, try printing the document and proofreading from the page. On top of this, change the font of the document. As mentioned before, making the work seem unfamiliar helps you to gain distance from it and, in turn, to be more critical of the quality.

Pay attention to the formatting guidelines

Students often express annoyance and confusion at the fact that different departments often have different referencing and formatting guidelines in place. In turn, markers often express annoyance and confusion that students have not adhered to clear formatting guidelines. It might seem awkward at first, but once you get into the habit of reading the formatting guidelines carefully before you start, and following them from the outset, it becomes much easier to adjust to different rules. On top of this, if you go on to postgraduate study, and have to write for publication, you'll find that different journals all have their own variations on formatting. It's good to get into the habit now of adhering to the rules as required.

Pay close attention to details such as which unit of measurement you should use, how to abbreviate terminology, and whether certain pieces of terminology need to be italicised. Making sure that you follow guidelines properly helps your work attain a higher standard, and looks more professional.

Conclusion

Editing and proofreading are integral to the recursive writing process, not last-minute additions just before the essay is handed in. As you can see, many of the ideas here refer back to previous discussions of structure and tone. Making sure that you carry out both processes properly will substantially improve the quality of your work. This chapter has offered strategies to ensure that you know how to thoroughly check every level of your work to make sure you do yourself justice in the final draft.

You should also consider editing and proofreading a way for you to provide feedback on your own work, giving you valuable information on your own writing habits. If possible, try to keep notes of the types of issues that require correction at the proofreading stage, and check these each time you have a new assignment. This should let you track progress in your writing throughout your degree.

15

Making the Most of Feedback

Why is feedback important?

Writing is part of learning. We've found that students have the tendency to treat each assignment as a discrete experience, instead of thinking reflectively about how their skills are developing over the course of their studies. This chapter will encourage you to think carefully about the feedback you receive on your written work, and how you can use it to shape your next assignment and develop as a writer.

By the time you have completed and submitted a piece of coursework, it can be difficult to be objective about your work. You've spent a lot of time researching this subject and planning and writing the assignment. As a result, you are very close to the topic. You are also likely to be very focused on what grade you are going to achieve, and what kind of feedback you might receive. When you get your assignments back, it can be tempting to simply look at the grade, read over the written feedback, and then set it aside before moving on to the next piece of coursework.

However, feedback is a valuable way for you to develop your skills and improve your grades at every stage in academic life, from first-year undergraduate level to PhD studies and professional academic life.

While we find that students are often keen to read the feedback on their assignments as soon as they get it back, we also find that students can often have a tendency to view each assignment in isolation, failing to recognise that the feedback they receive on one report can be useful for other pieces of work too.

Markers offer feedback in order to help you improve your work in the future. They not only look at your understanding of the subject content but also offer advice on skills they want you to develop throughout the course of your degree: the ability to summarise complex information; the ability to apply new knowledge to solve problems; the ability to evaluate approaches and methods; the ability to synthesise disparate pieces of information; and the ability to understand how your own work fits into a wider context. Demonstrating these abilities through your writing will determine your success in a variety of different assessment types: reports, dissertations, exams. Taking the time to read the feedback carefully and looking over your assignment with an objective eye will, therefore, help you to identify which areas you can strengthen for future assignments.

How to use feedback effectively

Before you look at your own assignment in more detail, you should make sure that you have a copy of the marking criteria for your subject. This will allow you to see what areas the marker will have focused on when they were assessing your work, and should also help you gain an understanding of the skills your marker wants you to exhibit and develop in your work. Standard areas might include: your ability to adhere to formal structure as well as present complex information in a logical, coherent manner; the depth of your understanding; your use of evidence, and your ability to demonstrate its relevance to the assignment purpose; the quality and breadth of your reading, and your ability to contextualise your own work within that; and so on.

Table 15.1 is an example of a typical marking scheme.

Level	Grade	Descriptor
Excellent	A	A well-written and well-structured answer which demonstrates a comprehensive level of knowledge. Full understanding of concepts. Data is clearly presented and fully discussed. References are used appropriately. Formatting guidelines have been followed. There might be some very minor issues present.
Very Good	B	A mostly well-written answer which demonstrates a wide knowledge of the subject, and evidence of additional reading. Good understanding of concepts. Data is mostly clearly presented and discussed in the context of wider literature. Formatting guidelines have been followed. There might be some minor issues present.
Good	C	The quality of the writing and structure is variable throughout. Knowledge is generally solid, and evidence of reading is present, although limited. Essential ideas are understood. Gaps or misunderstandings in the data, leading to flawed conclusions. Some errors in formatting. Overall, there is likely to be at least one major content issue (gap or misunderstanding).

Table 15.1   Typical marking scheme

Level	Grade	Descriptor
Satisfactory	D	Overall, work is limited in terms of understanding, reading and discussion. Gaps and errors in data. Evidence of additional reading, but limited, inappropriate, or misunderstood. Writing and structure occasionally erratic, leading to problems in communication. Several formatting problems.
Weak	E	Poorly written and structured. Understanding of basic concepts is poor, with serious flaws. Data misunderstood and poorly presented, with serious gaps. Reading limited. Very poorly formatted, with multiple referencing problems.
Poor	F	Lack of evidence of understanding of basic concepts and subject. Additional reading is severely limited and poorly grasped. Data is inappropriate and misunderstood. Very poorly written, with understanding inhibited as a result. Severe formatting and referencing errors.
Very Poor	G	No attempt made to answer question.
	H	Blank

Table 15.1 *(Continued)*

Now that you've familiarised yourself with the marking scheme, carefully read over your assignment again, thinking about those areas that the marking scheme specifically mentions. Try to imagine that it was written by someone else. Read it aloud (or ask someone else to read it aloud for you). Which section of the marking scale do you feel describes it best? Look back at Chapter 3, and consider why the marker set a specific task, and what you were being asked to demonstrate in this particular assignment. Have you demonstrated this? In our experience, students often demonstrate a disconnect between their understanding of what an assignment should be, what they produced, and the feedback they received. Bridging these gaps by reflecting on the whole process will help you understand the strengths and weaknesses of your work.

Now read over your work again, this time with this particular assessment in mind. In retrospect, were there any parts that you were uncertain about while you were writing? Or that you wish you'd been able to spend more time on? Are there any parts that you would change now that you have some distance from the assessment? Is this reflected in parts of the work which now perhaps seem a little weaker than the rest to you?

Now look at the grade and marker feedback again. Do you agree with it, now that you've read over your work with a clearer understanding of the marking criteria and reflected on your own work?

Although it might seem unnecessary, now that the work has been graded, it can be a valuable exercise to try to write these sections again, bearing in mind your new understanding: gained through understanding the marking criteria, through reading your marker's feedback, and through your own reflections on the process.

Look at *every* level of the work to see what could be improved. For example:

- Were your sentences too long, tacking important ideas together without giving you an opportunity to expand on them?
- Were there grammatical errors that might have confused your reader?
- Was your word choice imprecise, giving the impression that you didn't fully understand a concept, and preventing you from explaining it well?
- Was your paragraphing erratic, giving the impression that your thinking was incoherent?
- Did your work lack connectives, giving your reader the sense that your ideas were disconnected and without context?

This exercise will let you understand how to strengthen those areas which appeared weak, and will ensure that you get the maximum benefit from the whole experience. It will also boost your confidence by showing you that you do have the ability to write at the highest level expected by your marker. If you're still confused about the grade you have been given, then most tutors would be willing to discuss this in more detail. Tutors spend a lot of time marking, and like to know that students are reading their feedback carefully, and using it as a means to improve their work.

Moving on from the assignment, what steps can you take next to enhance the skills and understanding your marker was looking for?

The assessment of your subject understanding is obviously crucial. Try to do any extra reading that your marker might have recommended. You should speak to your course tutor or learning adviser if you are having difficulty grasping key concepts, or cannot see how/why your understanding is flawed.

You should also, however, consider broader skills. Even feedback which might seem to be entirely about your understanding of the content might have relevance for your writing skills. Did your writing make your explanation of a concept unclear, perhaps leading your marker to think that you didn't fully grasp the concept? Was your wording ambiguous? Was your description of a process overly wordy and poorly structured? How might you do things differently to avoid this in future?

Look back over the previous chapters of this book, especially those which relate to areas that your marker has identified as a strength or a weakness.

Peer review

Some university courses encourage a practice known as peer review.

Peer review is an activity which involves getting groups of students to assess each other's work, and offer feedback. This can be a very productive process. Looking at other students' work through a marker's eyes can help you to get a sense of what is considered a 'good' report, and why. You can then use this knowledge to inform your work, because you've put yourself in the marker's role, and now have a better idea of what they're looking for. This gives you greater control over the writing process, reinforcing the idea of an audience in your head from the outset.

Setting up an informal peer review group with other students on your course is a good way to help you understand and use the feedback you receive more effectively. It's often best to structure these sessions around a specific set of questions. Here's an example of a piece of work, and some questions that might be asked of it:

Describe the structures involved in memory and olfaction.

One of the reasons **(phrasing is a bit clumsy)** that smell **(is olfaction a better academic word to use here?)**, memory and emotion seem to be connected has to do with the structure of the brain (Wilson and Stevenson, 2003). The amygdala, olfactory complex, and hippocampus are all part of a larger structure known as the limbic system. **(should that have been the topic sentence?)** The amygdala, which is involved in processing memories to do with emotions such as fear and anger **(is that all it does?)**, plays an important role. It is located close to the primary olfactory complex, which deals with olfaction. The amygdala has direct connections to the hippocampus, which deals with short and long-term memory. It can be seen to be important, for survival reasons, that mammals develop and store memories to do with fear and anger. However, the idea that only one specific part of the brain, the limbic system, deals with these emotions has been contested by some neuroscientists (Heimer, 2007). **(should this be the beginning of a new paragraph?)**

(Adapted from Wilson and Stevenson, 2003; Heimer, 2007).

Box 15.1   Example of peer-reviewed paragraph

Remember to use the marking criteria, too. How would you assess this paragraph if you were to use the criteria we discussed earlier? Look at the same key areas that the marker would focus on: knowledge and understanding, evidence of wider reading, clear presentation of data. It might not be possible to judge all this in the excerpt we have here, but it still gives you a sense of the kind of questions that you should ask of your own work.

In this particular paragraph, for example, you could ask bigger skills-based questions, as well as the specific issues highlighted above. How effectively has the writer synthesised different ideas? Not very well, from the broken look of the structure. Have they presented complex information in a way that helps you to understand it?

Asking questions like these helps you clearly see how writing acts as an expression of your thinking. It might well be that this student does have a deep knowledge of these concepts, and understands how to synthesise them into a coherent understanding, *but their writing does not express this*. As their marker, you would only be able to grade them on the work they have presented you. This is why the structuring strategies we have discussed, from sentence structure to paragraphing, are vital tools in allowing you to demonstrate your abilities.

Put yourself in the marker's shoes again. What about this paragraph? What would you comment on? What wider observations might you make? A couple of comments have been made to start you off.

Discuss the neurological functions involved in the processing of music.

Attempting to understand how the brain deals with music is complex **(this topic seems really big)**. The frontal areas of the brain seem to be involved when music elicits an emotional response (Warren, 2008). The brains of musicians and non-musicians seem to deal with musical input differently. Parts of the brain which deal with issues such as motor tasks seem to exhibit structural changes. **(I don't see the link between these two sentences)** There are similarities in how the brain deals with music and how it deals with language. For example, Broca's area is implicated in both. Rhythm and tonality both involves complex processes crossing several different structures. When the rhythm is particularly complex, even more parts of the brain become involved, such as the cerebellum. Damage to the amygdala can affect the emotional perception of music, according to a study carried out by Gosselin, Peretz, Johnsen and Adolphs in 2007. Brain damage can impact on musical ability, depending on the part of the brain which is affected, and the role it performs in terms of musical ability.

(Adapted from Warren, 2008).

Box 15.2   Example of possible marker comments

Conclusion

We talked at the beginning of Chapter 12 about the nature of communication in written work. If we were reading a piece of your written work aloud to your tutor, then you would be able to get a decent sense, from facial expressions, how they felt about your work. If they seemed confused, you can adjust the speed or volume of your voice, or provide extra explanations, or analogies. They could ask a question outright if they wanted, and you could answer, reassuring them about any apparent problems with your work.

We cannot do this in the same way in an essay, or in a report. The conversation remains one-sided and oddly delayed until your work is graded and returned to you, at which point your reader can respond to what you've said.

You should regard the tutor/marker's feedback on your work, then, as a valuable contribution to the conversation. You can get the most from it by responding to it, as opposed to passively reading it. In turn, you can implement your improved understanding of what readers/markers are looking for when you are writing your process drafts.

Remember that feedback is not simply a judgment of your work, but also an opportunity to take control of your work and improve in future assessments. Using feedback in this way will ensure that you can extract the maximum benefit from it.

Table 15.2 shows a theoretical model of learning goals known as Bloom's taxonomy. It is widely used by teachers and tutors as a way of designing coursework and exams to help students work towards key educational goals. Look closely at it, and think back to the sample marking criteria, or your actual marking criteria. Think about the skills you employ when producing a piece of written work. Does it help you understand what markers want to see in your work, and what they value most?

Level 1 – Remember	The ability to recall and replicate facts
Level 2 – Understand	The ability to explain concepts
Level 3 – Apply	The ability to take existing information and apply it to a new problem
Level 4 – Analyse	The ability to draw connections between ideas, identify patterns, and identify similarities and differences
Level 5 – Evaluate	The ability to judge the value of something, based on objective analysis
Level 6 – Create	The ability to create new and original work through hypothesis or synthesis or investigation

Table 15.2 Bloom's taxonomy (Bloom, 1956)

Chapter 16

Conclusion

We started this book by expressing the hope that by giving you a thorough working knowledge of how scientific writing works, you would feel confident enough to take control of your writing, and see yourself as a scientific writer.

In order to do that, we led you through all the stages of producing a piece of written work, from deconstructing the question to dealing with feedback, providing background information along the way to help you understand how and why certain conventions are in place. Each section of the book, Understanding Scientific Writing, Preparing to Write, and Getting Down to Writing, was designed with practicality as the guiding principle: giving you information you could put into practice immediately.

Central to our approach is reminding you that writing is a two-way street, with you at one end, and your reader at the other. Writing is about communication. Keeping in mind the principles behind all forms of good communication, clarity, concision, and coherence should help you to build the foundation of the development of your own writing style.

We also want to stress that writing ability is not static. As you produce each new piece of written work, you will continue to develop as a writer. Remember, as we said, to reflect on the writing process, about what seems difficult, and what seems easy, and how to continue to improve. Look carefully at your feedback and use it as a way to move forward. Simply by engaging with the ideas in this book, you have already started to reflect on yourself as a writer, and laid the groundwork for further improvement.

Key

The comma – quiz

1 In order to ensure consistency, the same method of recording results was employed in each experiment.
2 It is suggested that this approach should not be employed, as this is an expensive, time-consuming technique.
3 The results obtained showed an increase, but this did not change our initial hypothesis.
4 Lithium, an alkali metal, is highly reactive.
5 The diatomic elements are: fluorine, chlorine, oxygen, hydrogen, nitrogen, bromine(,) and iodine.

The semicolon – quiz

1 Many studies omitted this detail; in fact, it is vital.
2 There were four important decisions made; the first seemed vital, but it did not impact results.
3 The results obtained showed an increase, but this did not change our initial hypothesis.
4 Lithium, an alkali metal, is highly reactive.
5 The diatomic elements are: fluorine, chlorine, oxygen, hydrogen, nitrogen, bromine(,) and iodine.
6 The results confirmed our initial thought; moreover, they confirmed the hypotheses of several other studies.

The colon – quiz

1 One key detail was omitted: time.
2 There were four important decisions made; the first seemed vital, but it did not impact results.
3 The results obtained showed a change in the following: temperature, mass, and reactivity.
4 The diatomic elements are: fluorine, chlorine, oxygen, hydrogen, nitrogen, bromine(,) and iodine.

Bibliography

Bear, M.F., Connors, B.W., Paradiso, M.A. 2016. *Neuroscience: exploring the brain*, 4th edition. Wolters Kluwer, Philadelphia, Pennsylvania.

Bloom, B. S.; Engelhart, M. D.; Furst, E. J.; Hill, W. H.; Krathwohl, D. R. (1956). *Taxonomy of educational objectives: The classification of educational goals. Handbook I: Cognitive domain*. 1st Edition. New York: David McKay Company.

Fox, M.A., Whitesell, J.K. 2004. *Organic Chemistry*. Jones & Bartlett Learning (s.l.).

Gaiman, N. 2013. *Introduction to Fahrenheit 451*, 60th Anniversary Edition. Harper Voyager, London.

Godfrey, J, 2013. *The Student Phrasebook: Vocabulary for Writing at University*, 1st Edition. Palgrave MacMillan, Houndmills, Basingstoke, Hampshire.

Goldacre, B. 2007. What's Wrong with Dr Gillian McKeith PhD? *Bad Science* [Online]. Available from: http://www.badscience.net/2007/02/ms-gillian-mckeith-banned-from-calling-herself-a-doctor/ [Accessed 30 September 2016].

Greetham, D.B. 2013. *How to Write Better Essays*, 3rd edition. Palgrave Macmillan, Houndmills, Basingstoke, Hampshire.

Heimer, L., Hoesen, G.W.V., M.D, M.T., Zahm, D.S. 2007. *Anatomy of Neuropsychiatry: The New Anatomy of the Basal Forebrain and Its Implications for Neuropsychiatric Illness*, 1st edition. Academic Press, Boston.

Liberati, A., Altman, D.G., Tetzlaff, J., Cynthia Mulrow, C., Gøtzsche, P.C., Ioannidis, J.P.A., Clarke, M., Devereaux, P.J., Kleijnen, J. and Moher, D. 2009. The PRISMA Statement for Reporting Systematic Reviews and Meta-Analyses of Studies that Evaluate Health Care Interventions: Explanation and Elaboration. *PLOS Medicine*, 6, e1000100.

McCrimmon, J.M. 1984. *Writing with a Purpose*, 8th edition. ed. Houghton Mifflin (s.l.).

Moher, D., Liberati, A., Tetzlaff, J., Altman, D.G., The Prisma Group, 2009. Preferred Reporting Items for Systematic Reviews and Meta-Analyses: The PRISMA Statement. *PLOS Medicine*, 6, e1000097.

Murray, D.M. 1972. *Teach Writing as a Process, Not Product. The Leaflet* 11–14.

Murray, R. 2011. *How to Write a Thesis*, 3rd edition. Open University Press, Maidenhead.

Pitkin, R.M., Branagan, M.A. and Burmeister, L.F. 1999. Accuracy of Data in Abstracts of Published Research Articles. *JAMA*, 281, 1110–1111.

Pitkin, R.M. and Branagan, M.A., 1998. Can the accuracy of abstracts be improved by providing specific instructions? A randomized controlled trial. JAMA, 280, 267–269.

Sezonov, G., Joseleau-Petit, D. and D'ari, R. 2007. Escherichia coli Physiology in Luria-Bertani Broth. *Journal of Bacteriology*, 189, 8746–8749.

Sollaci, L.B. and Pereira, M.G., 2004. The introduction, methods, results, and discussion (IMRAD) structure: a fifty-year survey. *Journal of the Medical Library Association*, 92, 364–71.

Sprat, T. 1667. *The History of the Royal Society of London, for the Improving of Natural Knowledge*, London.

Van Noorden, R. 2014. Publishers withdraw more than 120 gibberish papers. *Nature News* [Online]. Available from: http://www.nature.com/news/publishers-withdraw-more-than-120-gibberish-papers-1.14763/ [Accessed 30 September 2016].

Warren, J. 2008. How does the brain process music? *Clinical Medicine* 8, 32–36.

Watson, C., Kirkcaldie, M., Paxinos, G. 2010. *The Brain: An Introduction to Functional Neuroanatomy*, 1st edition. Academic Press, Boston.

Webelements [online resource] (http://www.webelements.com/)

Williams, K., Reid, M., 2011. *Time Management*. Palgrave Macmillan, New York.

Wilson, D.A., Stevenson, R.J. 2003. The fundamental role of memory in olfactory perception. *Trends in Neuroscience.* 26, 243–247.

World Health Organisation [online resource] (http://www.who.int/en/)

Index